STRAIGHT

IN THE

ARMY

A Novel by:

MAURICE HALL BUCHANAN

Gotham Books

30 N Gould St.
Ste. 20820, Sheridan, WY 82801
https://gothambooksinc.com/

Phone: 1 (307) 464-7800

Published by Gotham Books (October 16, 2024)

ISBN: 979-8-88775-787-2 (H)
ISBN: 979-8-88775-785-8 (P)
ISBN: 979-8-88775-786-5 (E)

Because of the dynamic nature of the Internet, any web addresses or links contained in this book may have changed since publication and may no longer be valid.

ACKNOWLEDGEMENT

I want to thank my sister Annette Buchanan for her assistance in making this book. She helped with the editing and research and this book would not have been possible without her help.

TABLE OF CONTENTS

PROLOGUE

June 26, 2015

A silver Lexus pulled into the driveway of a large two-story colonial building. A sign on the front walkway read, "Old Shady Lakes Home". A tall, thin, lanky man about fifty-five years of age stepped out of the vehicle. He wore round rimless glasses and a tan fedora. He took off his hat and wiped the sweat from his forehead with a handkerchief. His dark hair was thinning at the top; his glasses continuously slid down his thin nose, and he would slide them back up to the bridge. He carried a tape recorder and had a camera on a strap around his neck. He slowly walked up the stairs, exhausted from the long journey from the city. He acknowledged an elderly woman sitting on a rocking chair, looking in the distance.

"Hello, ma'am," he said, tipping his hat. "I'm looking for Walter Jenkins. I have an appointment with him."

The woman said nothing, her eyes fixed in the distance. He continued into the building and saw a nurse sitting behind a desk. He walked up to the nurse and smiled.

"Hello, nurse. I'm Joseph Shapiro. I believe Walter Jenkins is expecting me."

"Oh yes, you're his two o'clock appointment. Follow me."

He followed the nurse down a hallway filled with elderly people. One man was slowly walking while pulling an IV stand next to him. Another was in a wheelchair, and some were using walkers. He followed her to the end of the hallway; the door was already open, and they walked in. An orderly with a washing pan in his hand and a short, chubby, blond nurse were talking to an older gentleman sitting in a wheelchair, who he assumed was Walter Jenkins. He appeared to be in his late eighties or early nineties. His head was bald at the top, with short, stubby, white hair on the sides. He had a cane resting on his lap and a hearing aid in one ear. He had a dark-brown complexion, and the whites of his eyes were yellow. The nurse stood firmly over him, her finger pointing down at him.

"Now you listen here, Mr. Jenkins. You stop giving Mr. Henry a hard time and let him do his job and bathe you."

"No!" Walter shouted, waving his cane in the air. "I will not have him bathe me." He looked at Joseph Shapiro, who was standing next to the nurse. "What kind of man gives another man a bath? He seems to like his job too much for a guy making only ten bucks an hour. I want a woman to give me a bath. She can be young, old, pretty, or ugly; it doesn't matter, just as long as she's a female."

"All right, if you want to be stubborn, so be it. You just won't have a bath, that's all. Come on Mr. Henry."
The nurse quickly glanced at Mr. Shapiro before storming out the room, followed by the orderly.
Shapiro walked over to Walter and extended his hand.

"Hello, Mr. Jenkins, I'm Joseph Shapiro from Stabler Books." They shook hands.

"Oh yes," said Walter, I've been expecting you. You're that writer who's going to do a story on me."

"Not just you, Mr. Jenkins, but your whole battalion."

"Well, have a seat," said Walter.

"You know, maybe I should come back at a more convenient time."

"No, now is as good a time as any," said Walter, gesturing for Shapiro to sit down. Shapiro sat nervously on the bed. He placed the tape recorder next to him. He shifted his glasses back on the bridge of his nose.

"Maybe it would be better if someone else did this interview."

"Why? You're already here," said Walter.

"Mr. Jenkins, you seem to be a homophobe. Now I'm going to be truthful with you and let you know right up front that I'm gay. Maybe it would be more comfortable for you and me if someone else interviewed you. We have other qualified writers in our agency."

Walter squinted his eyes as he looked at him more closely.

"On the contrary, Mr. Shapiro. I think you will do just fine."

"Are you sure, Mr. Jenkins? It's important that you feel comfortable with the person who's interviewing you. There are only a handful of the all-black 761st Tank Battalion left, and I want us to have an honest dialogue with each other, with neither of us feeling uncomfortable."

"You'll do just fine, Mr. Shapiro."

Shapiro took out his pen and pad and turned on the tape recorder. He took out the mike and placed it closer to Walter. Walter positioned his wheelchair facing Mr. Shapiro.

"Where should I begin?" Walter asked.

"Why don't we start from the very beginning, before you got your draft notice."

Walter leaned back in his wheelchair, stared in the distance, and started talking.

CHAPTER 1

October 1942

I was awakened by the clip-clop sound of a horse walking along the pavement outside my Harlem apartment. I got out of bed to look outside. It was a brisk, sunny autumn morning. Down below, there was an old Jewish man riding a horse-drawn wagon and collecting junk. A sign at the side of the wagon read, "Give junk to help our boys overseas." The wagon slowly made its way down the street. Every now and then, the old man dismounted his wagon and looked over discards left at the side of the road.

You don't hear that sound anymore, I thought – the clip-clop sound a horse makes when it's walking along the pavement. I remember when I was a kid growing up, I would hear that sound all the time, back in the day when horses shared the road with automobiles. Today it's mostly automobiles. You seldom see a horse-drawn wagon, or a horse for that matter.

The smell of breakfast, cooking in the kitchen wafted into my room. I put on my bathrobe and made my way to the kitchen.

My father was sitting at the table with breakfast in front of him, reading the morning paper. The front page read: "Hitler's War Machine Stalled in Stalingrad." I was surprised to see my father up so early in the morning. At this time, he was usually at his night job, working the graveyard shift as a night watchman at the docks. He would sometimes come home late in the morning, around ten o' clock, long after I had gone to work. He was a stocky built man, did not have an ounce of fat on him. He attributed it to hard work in the cane fields in Jamaica. He was fifty-two and spoke with a slight accent, which became heavy when he got excited. My mother was a slim, light-skinned woman who was mixed - Negro with a little

1

Indian and some Chinese. They both made their way to America during the Roaring Twenties, right before the Great Depression. My father once told me that I was conceived in Jamaica but born here in America, making me a US citizen. He always told me that I was truly Jamaican.

"How come you're not at work, Dad?" I asked.

"They gave me the night off – nothing of value to watch over. Those German U boats are causing hell out there. Hopefully there will be work tomorrow."

The German submarines were causing problems in the Atlantic, sinking cargo ships with supplies en-route to England. It was desperate times for England.

"I'm sure there will be, dear," said my mother. She put her hand on my shoulder. "Would you like some breakfast, Walter?" she asked.
"What are you having?"
"Ackee and saltfish."

"No thanks, I'm not hungry."

"How about some tea?"

"I'll just have a cup of coffee," I said. I didn't feel like eating ackee that morning. My father lowered his newspaper and looked at me with a surprised look.

"Coffee?" he asked. "How long have you been drinking coffee?"

"About a year." My mother placed a cup of coffee in front of me.

"Kids sure do grow up fast," he said. It seems like only yesterday you were drinking cocoa."

"Where have you been?" I said jokingly. My father continued reading the newspaper while I sipped my coffee.

"So how is the war effort?" I asked.

"Those Germans bit off more than they could chew. They got pushed back from Moscow. Now they're bogged down in Stalingrad. Those Russians are giving them a run for their money." He looked at me as I continued to sip my coffee. "You know, you're lucky that you didn't qualify for the draft because of that hole in your heart."

I sipped some more coffee and continued to gaze at the back of his newspaper. "Sometimes I feel guilty when I see people my age in uniform and I'm not," I said. "People sometimes give me a dirty look when I'm walking down the street in my civilian clothes."

"*Me nuh care wha' dem tink*," my father said in the thick Jamaican accent that he got whenever he got excited. "*Yu a mi only son; yu nuh 'ave nuh bizniz a go fight nuh war. Dat a white man's war.*"

I didn't want to discuss this anymore with my father, so I quickly finished the last of my coffee and excused myself and went to the bathroom. I took a quick bath, got dressed and hurried out the door for work. I took a bus, then a train to my job at the Waldorf Hotel in downtown New York. It was a luxurious hotel with beautiful carpeting and grand crystal chandeliers. I was lucky to get a job there, fresh out of high school and during the Depression. I had started out as a dish washer and worked my way up to waiter.

I was about five minutes late when I walked in, so I quickly put on my white shirt and apron to start the morning shift.
"Good morning, Walter," the cook said.
"Good morning, Mr. Bob," I replied. I was about ready to serve breakfast when the head waiter motioned for me to come over. "Yes, Mr. Sheppard?"

"The boss wants to see you."

"For what?" I asked.

"I dunno. Get over there. I'll cover for you."

I walked into my boss's office. I was nervous about being called in. What could it be? I thought. Am I going to be laid off, or is he upset because I'm late? He was talking on the phone when I walked in, and he gestured for me to sit down. His office was not as immaculate as the hotel; it was mid-sized, with two gray file cabinets in a corner. He had a small fan on his desk and a black and white picture of a woman who I assumed was his wife, with two teenage girls standing behind her. He finished speaking on the phone and placed it on the cradle. He put his elbows on the desk and folded his hands, then placed his chin on top.

"Good morning, Walter."

"Good morning, Mr. Riley. Look, if it's about me being late, I--"

"No, it's not about that. Besides, you're seldom late. You heard about Mr. Sheppard leaving, haven't you?"

"No, I haven't. He's leaving?"

"Yup. Got drafted in the Navy. Tomorrow is his last day."

"That's too bad," I replied.

"I'm looking for someone to replace him as head waiter. The job is yours if you want it."

"Me?" I exclaimed excitedly.

"Yes, you." Mr. Riley smiled. "You've been here four years now, and you've been doing good work. I personally think you can handle it. So, do you want the job?"

My heart leapt with joy. I did all I could to contain my excitement.

"Yes! Thank you, sir. Thank you so much."

"Mr. Sheppard will start training you today. When he leaves, you'll be on your own." I stood and briskly shook his hand.
"Thanks, Mr. Riley. I won't let you down."

"I'm sure you won't, Walter. You're a good worker. Good luck."

I walked out of his office elated; I was walking on air. The rest of the day, Mr. Sheppard showed me the procedures of being a head waiter. He was a slim white man with dark features, and he had a stern manner about him. He handled us waiters with an authoritarian manner and was strict. Most of the waiters were Negro and resented him. I planned on being a little easier with the guys, not because I wanted to change things but because that's the way I am, more easygoing. I finished my shift and took the elevated train back home to Harlem. I was looking out the train window and remembered how, when I was a child growing up, I was afraid of riding the train because it was so high in the air, and I had images in my head of the train falling from the tracks. As I grew older, I got used to it and no longer feared riding.

The train was packed with the usual rush-hour crowd. I was standing, holding the arm rail, admiring the view of the city. An obese man with a briefcase pushed his way through the crowd to get off at his stop and brushed right by me without excusing himself. It didn't faze me, because I was still on cloud nine. As the train passed familiar buildings, I noticed the gym where I worked out. I had been taking boxing lessons for about a year, and although I didn't have the talent to go pro, the training helped me to be focused and disciplined. My trainer was reluctant about me joining the boxing team on account of my heart condition, but a letter from my doctor stating that I would be fine as long as I didn't overdo it convinced him to let me join. As the train rolled to a stop, the crowd thinned out as a group of riders exited. I saw an empty seat and rushed to get it. I sat next to the window, smiling. I still couldn't believe that I got promoted to head-waiter. I get to supervise and direct the other waiters, I'd get 50 percent of all the tips, and I'd get paid more per hour. With tips, I'd be making more than my father.

The train squeaked to a stop at the station and I exited. I went down the stairs and walked along Lennox Avenue. The Harlem Renaissance was dying out, becoming obsolete. I remember when I was a young teenager, the Harlem streets would be blaring with jazz music. There were jazz clubs, after-hour joints, and speakeasies up and down the avenue. The speakeasies had become a thing of the past since they repealed Prohibition, but the night clubs and after-hour joints were still around, although not as many as during their height in the thirties.

My girlfriend Gwen worked in Toby's, one of the nightclubs. It was owned and operated by a man named Toby Williams. He had bought out a man named Goodman, who had previously named the place the Crystal Shack. Gwen had worked at the Crystal Shack then stayed when Toby took over. She was a cocktail waitress with a fine figure. We had been going out with each other for about six months. I walked into the club; there was light saxophone music playing in the background, with cigarette smoke drifting and disappearing in the air. It was the middle of the week, so the crowd was light and scattered. I checked with the bartender, who was washing glasses at the sink, and he told me that Gwen was not scheduled to work for another hour. So, I decided to go to a record store to buy Louis Armstrong's latest album. As I was leaving the store, I saw Gwen walking down the street. She was about to enter Toby's when I caught her attention.
"Walter? What are you doing here?" she asked. "I thought this was your night at the gym."

"I was about to go to the gym, but I thought I'd come by to talk."

"Not now, Walter – I'm going to be late."

"I couldn't hold back any longer and decided to get to the point. "I got a promotion at my job," I said.

"You what!" she exclaimed.

"You are looking at the new head waiter."

"What happened to Mr. Sheppard?"

"He got drafted in the military."

"That's great, Walter! Well, not so great for Mr. Sheppard, but great for you."

"I thought maybe we could celebrate. When do you get off?"

She placed her hands on her hips and put on a cute, sensuous smile - the smile I always found appealing. She thought for a moment. "I get off at midnight, which would be too late to do any celebrating."

"No," I replied, with a mischievous smile on my face. "The night will still be young."

"All right, then, midnight it is." She gave me a quick kiss on the lips, then rushed off to her job.

I walked the rest of the way to my parents' apartment complex. I cut through the alleyway and darted up the back stairwell. I opened the door to the kitchen. My mother was usually cooking, but there was no sign of food being cooked or her. I went to the adjoining room to find her sitting on the sofa in the living room, with my father standing beside her.

"I have great news," I announced. I still couldn't contain my excitement. Then I noticed my mother's eyes were puffy and red from crying.
"What's wrong?" I asked, quickly walking toward them.

My father held up a letter from the president of the United States.

"You've been drafted."

CHAPTER 2

I sat at the kitchen table, depressed, and stared at the letter sent to me from the State Department. It read:

Greetings,

Having submitted yourself to a local board of your neighbors for the purpose of determining your availability for training and service in the land or naval forces of the United States, you are hereby notified that you have been selected for training and service therein.

I couldn't believe this was happening to me. This morning I was on top of the world, in high spirits, only to be knocked down. I had a beautiful girlfriend, a promotion at my job. Things were going well, but now lost because of some damn war across the ocean.

"Didn't they turn you down because of a heart condition? Why are they sending you a draft notice?" my father asked.

"I don't know," I replied, still dazed. "I'll go down tomorrow and straighten this matter out."

"I'm not going to stand for it. You're my only son. I'm not going to have them take you away to get killed. This is a white man's war, and I don't want you getting involved," he said in his thick Jamaican accent.

My mother walked over and placed her hand on my shoulder. Her eyes were still puffy and red from crying. "Son, me and your father were talking and thought maybe it would be a good idea for you to go to Jamaica. We have relatives there who would be glad to take you in."

"For how long?"

For as long as it takes," said my father. He had a bottle of over proof Jamaican rum on the table. He poured himself a drink and took a long pull. I don't know how my father could drink that stuff straight. He lowered his head, then raised it and looked me straight in the eyes.

"Look, son. Your mother and I are both Jamaican. You were born here, but there is a law in
Jamaica that states that if both parents are from the island, their offspring are eligible to be
Jamaican citizens. Now, the law says that you have to be eighteen, and you're twenty-two, but I'm sure I can work something out. I just have to know who to pay off."

"I don't think so, Dad. I'm an American. I don't think I would fit in over there. Besides, there are Jamaicans fighting in that war too."

"Yes, but it's all voluntary. There's no draft over there," he retorted.

"All right, I'll tell you what. Let me go down to the draft board and see what happens. I'm sure this is all just a mistake. I have a heart condition, so I won't be able to pass the medical exam."

My father took another drink of his rum, then sat heavily in the chair. He looked again at the morning newspaper that had been lying on the kitchen table. "Okay. You go down to the draft board and see what happens, but if things don't get straightened out, I'm going to contact your Aunt Beatrice in Jamaica."

CHAPTER 3

The next morning, I reported to the draft board. I took a written test, then went through a medical and psychological exam. Later that afternoon, I was shocked to find that I was fit for duty. I met with a recruiter later in his office. There were about eight desks with recruiters sitting behind them, with candidates sitting opposite them. I was led by a female soldier into the room. I could hear the clattering of typewriters in the background. A black recruiter was free. The soldier pointed him out to me and I strolled over to him. He was a staff sergeant, with a thin mustache and bald head. He was filling out paperwork when he saw me. He pointed to the chair on the other side of his desk.

"Have a seat," he said. I sat down and handed him my paperwork. He thumbed through it, glanced at me, then continued studying the papers. "You did pretty well on your written," he said. I nodded my head, still mildly stunned that I was there. "Just what kind of work do you want to do in the military?" he asked.

"Look, sir I don't –"

"Don't call me sir. I'm a sergeant. I work for a living." He laughed, then saw I didn't see the humor.

"You'll understand what I mean once you've been here for a while," he said.

"But that's what I don't understand, sergeant. I have a heart condition. The last time I was here, I was rejected for it."

"You were?" He went through the paperwork once again. "Oh yes, the last time you were here you had a three-centimeter hole in your heart. The x-rays show it went down to one centimeter, which is acceptable."

"So, you're saying the hole in my heart is smaller?"

"Yes, it is," he said beaming. "Which makes you fit for duty. Congratulations."

I sulked in my chair; the only one who seemed to be happy was the sergeant sitting across from me. I guess he felt that I should have been excited about being accepted, but I was not.

"So just what is it you want to do in the army?" he asked again.

"I was a dish washer for two years, then I got promoted to waiter. I just became the head waiter before I got my draft notice."

The recruiter looked at a list of options.

"Well, we need cooks," he said.

"I'll take it." I said. Being a cook sounded like it would be safer for me. I would be in the rear, behind enemy lines, I thought.

"Now hold on just a minute there, son. They're starting an all-Negro tank battalion. With your test score, you qualify."

"I don't know about that. Being a cook sounds more like what I'm qualified for."

"Come on, young man. Negro cooks are a dime a dozen. You have a chance to be a part of something that our race can be proud of." He stood up. He was a muscular middle-aged man with thick biceps. He walked over to the front of his desk and sat at the edge, in front of me. He looked around the room to make sure no one was listening, then lowered his voice so only I could hear him. His eyes bore into me as he looked me straight in the eye.

"I'm going to tell you something Negro to Negro. They say we don't have the smarts to handle a tank, that all we're capable of doing is cooking and digging ditches for latrines. But we have a chance to prove them wrong. *You* have the chance to prove them wrong."

"That all sounds good, sergeant, but if I'm in the tank battalion, won't I be out on the front lines?"

He folded his huge arms and looked at me. "Is that what you're afraid of?"

"It's not a matter of being afraid. I'm a pacifist at heart."

"That's just another word for scared," he said, smiling. He unfolded his arms and sat back behind his desk. "No need to worry about that. They're not going to send that unit overseas anytime soon."

"How can you be so sure?" I asked.

"It's common knowledge around here that they're not going to send an all-black tank battalion over on the front lines. We have to take this one step at a time. First, we have to prove to them that we can operate a tank just as good as a white soldier, then we prove to them that we can fight just as good. Are you willing to take that first step?" I didn't say a word. I just sat there contemplating what he just said.

"You will be doing your country a great service, not to mention your race. What are you going to tell your grandchildren? That you cooked a mean omelet in the mess hall or that you were one of the first members of an all-black tank battalion?"

CHAPTER 4

"You did what?" my father shouted.

"I joined the army, an all-black tank battalion," I said.

"I thought we talked about this last night. We were going to call your Aunt Beatrice in Jamaica."

"We talked about it, but I didn't agree to it."

My father was standing over the kitchen table. He had just come in from his watchman's job across town. He still had his flashlight and punch clock. My mother was sitting at the kitchen table, sipping a cup of tea.

"Are you sure this is what you want to do, dear?" she asked.

"You can never be one hundred percent sure of anything, Mom, but I'm pretty sure." Deep inside I was hoping I was making the right decision.

"Son, I don't think you know what you're getting yourself into. You're going to get yourself killed, and for what? A power struggle over in Europe? What business is this of yours? Do as I ask, son. Go to Jamaica until this war blows over."

"And do what?" I asked. "Be a citizen in another country? I'm already a citizen here."

"A second-class citizen is what you are?" my father replied.

"I already made up my mind, Dad. It's for the best."

My father walked over to me and held my shoulders, something he hadn't done since I was a kid. "Look, I'm just looking out for you like a father should. I don't want to see anything happen to you." He shook his head in frustration. Why did you have to join a tank battalion? They're the first to go on the front lines."

"The recruiter assured me that we are not going overseas. We'll be stationed down south somewhere."

"Don't believe what they tell you. They'll tell any kind of lie to get you in that unit."

"It's too late, Dad, I already took the oath. They're coming by in the morning to pick me up."

My father released his hands from my shoulders and sauntered over to the kitchen table. He slowly sat down beside my mother. He looked defeated, appearing not to grasp what I was saying. My mother was staring into her cup of tea, with tears in her eyes that threatened to drop at any minute. Why don't they understand? I thought. I'm a man and I have to do what I think is right for me. Why is this so difficult?

"And what about your job?" my father asked, his voice sounding hoarse.

"I already spoke with Mr. Riley, he told me my job will be waiting for me when I get back."

Both my mother and father were at a loss for words. They couldn't think of any other reason why I shouldn't go in the tank battalion or in the army. I was doing no good staying in the apartment, so I decided to go out and say good-bye to some friends.

"I'm going out for a while, Mom and Dad. I'll be back before eleven."

They both remained silent, sitting at the kitchen table. I went outside and walked over to Toby's, greeting some locals as I made my way over. I saw the bouncer, Country, at the door talking with Gwen.

"Hey, Country," I said. What's shaking, man?"

Country had a short haircut around the sides, with a part in the middle on top. He had thick biceps and huge hands. Rumors had it that he used to be a street fighter, and a good one at that. He knew that I had taken up boxing at the local gym and would give me some pointers.

"Hey, what's going on, Walter?" We shook hands.

"Hello, Gwen."

Gwen stared at me for a moment.

"I'm not speaking to you," she said.

I was surprised by her response. "What did I do?"

"You stood me up last night. You said you were going to take me out to celebrate your promotion and you never showed up. Not even a phone call."

I slapped my forehead.

"I'm sorry, baby, I completely forgot. So much has happened since we last talked. Come on,
    let's get a table and I'll explain."

Gwen hesitated. She was still upset.

"Go on, Gwen," said Country. "At least find out what he has to say."

She hesitated again for a second. "Oh, all right," she said. "I want to hear what kind of an excuse you have."

I took her hand, and Country led us to a nice isolated table in the corner. She was wearing a light-blue dress with a slit at the side and a black veiled hat. Her perfume smelled nice, and her figure looked good, as always. A waiter came over to take our order. After the waiter left, Gwen looked at me stoically. "Well, what happened?" she asked.

I explained everything to her: How I got drafted and passed the medical exam. How I joined the all-new Negro tank battalion. How I had to leave the next day. She looked at me in disbelief.

"I can't believe this all happened right after your promotion. That's a crying shame. And now you're going to be driving one of those tanks. That sounds awfully dangerous." She held out both of her hands and clasped my hand on the table. "I'm going to worry about you, baby. You be careful."

It was kind of nice seeing her worry about me like that. I considered telling her that they had no intention of sending a Negro tank unit over to fight. But I kind of liked seeing her this way, so caring.

"Don't worry, Gwen, I'll be careful. I feel that I have to do my duty and fight that Nazi war machine." I knew it was a bunch of bull I was talking, and I hoped that I wasn't laying it on too thick.

"You're so brave," she said. "I'm going to write you every day. And I promise I'll wait for you."

The waiter returned with our drinks and placed them on the table. She had red wine and I had a whiskey sour. The owner of the club, Toby, came walking over.

"Is everything okay?" he asked.

"Toby, Walter is going in the army. He's going to be in an all-black tank unit." Gwen repeated what I had just told her. She seemed so proud of me. She didn't stop beaming, and I didn't stop her from talking.

Toby looked surprised. He pulled out a chair and sat at our table.

"An All-Negro tank unit?" he asked. Are you kidding me? I didn't know we had one of those."

"It's a new battalion that the government is starting," I answered.

"When are you leaving?"

"Tomorrow."

"Well, I'll be." Toby snapped his fingers and a waiter instantly came over.

"Yes, Mr. Toby?"

"I want this man sitting here to have the best champagne we have, on the house."

The waiter rushed off to get the order. Toby was a medium-built man in his early thirties. He wore glasses and had a baby face. He wore a nice conservative business suit and matching tie. He reached in his inside pocket for a box of cigars. He offered one to me, but I declined. He lit his cigar nice and evenly around the edges, puffing on the end to get it started. He blew out the smoke, and then smiled at me.

"So, how long are you going in for?" he asked.

"Three years."

"Three years, huh? Well, don't worry about it, my man, those three years will fly by. Before you know it, you'll be back here having drinks with us."

The waiter returned with the bottle of champagne and glasses. He nodded his head in my direction and then quickly left to serve other customers.

Toby poured a drink for Gwen and me, then himself. We all raised our glasses.

"To you, Walter. May God be with you, and may you return home safely."

Some of the patrons in the club knew me from the neighborhood and came over to wish me luck on my tour of duty. More drinks were bought, and there was a lot of handshaking, backslapping, and farewells. Billie Holiday was scheduled to sing at the club in a couple of days, and I was disappointed that I would not be able to see her. I was a big fan of hers, and Toby knew it.

"I'll tell you what," he said. "I'll be sure to get an autographed picture of her for you."

"Would you?" I looked at him to see if he was really serious. "I would really appreciate it." Others had come by, and some were hanging around our table. After a brief celebration, Toby stood up. "All right, everybody. Why don't we leave this couple alone? I'm sure that Gwen and Walter would like some privacy."

There was some laughter as the well-wishers got up from the table. There were more "farewells" and "good lucks" before they melted into the crowded night club. A jazz band whose name I can't remember started playing the latest jazz music. The patrons got up on the dance floor and started dancing. They were doing the jitterbug and the Lindy hop. Gwen and I watched for a minute. I began to tap my foot and was getting in the mood to dance.

"You want to dance?" I asked.

"No, I have something better in mind. Let's get out of here," she said with a smile. I knew what that meant, and I quickly changed my mind about dancing. We gathered our things and walked toward the exit. She decided to go in the ladies' room to powder her nose. As I was waiting, a middle-aged man approached me.

"Hello, son. You remember me?"

I took a closer look at him.

"Oh yeah. You're Mr. Francis. How you doing?"

Mr. Francis was an old friend of my father's ever since I could remember. I remembered a talk he had with my father when I was a child, about his tour of duty in France during World War I. How he hardly experienced prejudice from the French people while stationed there. I was hiding under the table and they did not know I was there. He spoke of French women and whorehouses, and sex. I sat under the table flabbergasted by what they were talking about.

"I'm doing fine," Mr. Francis said. How's your father?"

"He's doing fine."

"I heard about you going in the army."

"Yes. I leave tomorrow."

"I was in the army back in 1917, stationed in France. I saw some action."

"Yes, I know."

"Did you know that I was in the infantry? I saw things no man should see, never mind a kid. It's not glorious son, it's ugly."

"Did my father send you?" I asked. I was thinking that my father had sent him to change my mind.
"No, he didn't. I heard from some neighbors. This kind of news travel fast around here." He put on his old fedora. "Take my advice, son. When the shooting starts, make sure you keep your head down." He walked out the door just as Gwen was coming out of the ladies' room.

"Who was that?" she asked.

"Nobody, just a friend of my father's."

We left the club and hailed a cab. We took it to a halfway decent hotel on Lenox Avenue and made love. We had done it a couple of times before, but this time it was different. It was more intense and passionate. After we finished, we lay next to each other, exhausted. I looked at her and reminisced about how we first met. She was working one night as a cocktail waitress at Toby's, and I called her over to order a pack of cigarettes. We had a bit of a conversation and she went about her business. Every night after that, I would order cigarettes or a drink and the conversations got longer. One night I asked her out on a date, she accepted, and we'd been together ever since. Though she was six years older than me, it never mattered. My mom and dad met her a couple of times, and they didn't seem to care for her much, but it didn't matter to me. What mattered was what I felt in my heart.

"Did you really mean what you said?" I asked.

"About what?"

"About waiting for me."

"Of course, sugar. I love you. You just make sure you come back in one piece."

"I love you too, sweetheart. When I get back, we'll be together again, forever."

Gwen looked at me.

"Is that a marriage proposal?" she asked.

I thought about it for a moment and realized how much this woman meant to me. Even though we hadn't been together for that long, I really loved her. She inspired me to be a better man. I felt like she was a part of me. I hated that I was leaving for the army, but this was a great opportunity and a chance to build something special for us.

"Yes, it is," I said with a smile on my face. "Do you accept?"

"Yes, yes, yes!" she shouted.

CHAPTER 5

I arrived at Camp Upton, New York, at 7:30 p.m. the next day. There were thousands of army recruits in the area. Most of the recruits on post were from all over the Northeast: New York, Boston, Philadelphia, Detroit, Washington D.C., and many other cities. When we arrived, the bus was integrated. When we exited, they began separating us into groups – white men in one formation and Negroes in the other. They marched the Negro soldiers to the end of the base, isolating us from the main post. Black soldiers could only go to the Post Exchange on certain days. For the first couple of weeks, we lived in dilapidated tents where we received haircuts, uniforms, and basic gear. We learned military courtesy and how to march in formation. We also received training in close-order drills and military decorum.

They kept us busy most days, but we found ourselves with a great deal of time on our hands at the end of our training while waiting for our orders to come through. So, we had time to form baseball and boxing teams and have tournaments. It was fun playing baseball, but I especially enjoyed boxing. I had some knowledge of boxing, since I trained at the local gym in Harlem, and I didn't mind passing down what I learned to the other men. More Negro soldiers were interested in boxing since Joe Louis had become heavy-weight champion of the world.

One day I stayed a little longer than I should have at the gym. After breakfast, I thought I'd go to the gym for some quick training. I was pounding away on the punching bag when I realized I was late for morning formation. The sergeants weren't too happy when I came walking into formation late. I drew two days of K.P. duty in the mess hall for that little stunt. I was in the kitchen washing pots and pans, which reminded me of my days working at the Waldorf Hotel. When I finished with the pots and pans, I was instructed by the sergeant to start peeling potatoes. I began peeling them with a knife, when a red-headed soldier sat next to me to help. As he peeled potatoes, he kept glancing over at me.

"Don't I know you?" he asked.

I stopped peeling and looked at him more closely.

"Wait a minute. You're Red, the saxophone player, right?"

"Me in the flesh," he said. I didn't recognize you at first with that haircut." We both laughed at the way we looked with our new haircuts.

Red was a white saxophone player who often played the Harlem circuit. He would play in clubs all over New York, and he once told me he liked playing in Harlem. It was good training, he said. He was a slim man in his early thirties, with red hair and freckles.

"Walter, right?"

I nodded. "Yeah, that's me."
"So, you joined the army?"

"No, I was drafted."

"I remember the last time I saw you. It was last month at Toby's."

"Yeah, I was there the night before I left. So how is Toby?" I asked.

"He's doing fine. He's getting a lot of business from military personnel passing through New York. So, how's that fine-looking girl friend of yours?"

"She's doing well. We're going to get hitched."

"Well, congratulations! When's the big day?"

"As soon as I get out."

Just then the mess sergeant strolled in. "Hey, you two!" he shouted. "A little less yapping and
a little more peeling. Come on, let's go!"

"Yes, sergeant!" we stated in unison.

I finished putting the potatoes in a giant pot and was carrying them over for the cook, when Red said, "Hey Walter, I got a weekend pass. Let's say we hook up and have a few beers. We can relive old times."

"Sounds good to me," I said.

"Hey!" the sergeant shouted. "I said knock it off! Come on, let's go. Move it! Move it!"

CHAPTER 6

That weekend, Red and I met outside the post. We managed to get a cab and rode into the next town. There was a small club patronized by mostly white soldiers. We had a few beers and talked about jazz, the club circuit and our old circle of friends.

"I wanted to join a year ago," said Red.

I looked at him in disbelief and almost choked on my beer. "You mean you volunteered for
this?"

"Yeah. After the Japs bombed Pearl Harbor, I felt it was my civic duty to join and fight for my country. I chickened out a couple of times, but I finally worked up the nerve to join. Didn't you want to join before you got drafted."

"Absolutely not!" I said.

Red and I were working on our fourth beer when a white soldier approached the bar. He was a tall, lanky fellow in need of a shave. He causally looked at Red. "Hey, Red," he said, "me and some of the boys are going to a nightclub about two miles from here - the Blue Fox. You want to join us?" Red quickly introduced me to the soldier. His name was Tim. We shook hands, then Tim turned his attention back to Red. "So, what do you say, Red? You want to come along?"

"I don't know," said Red.

"Come on, Red. The owner of the club said he heard you play the saxophone back in New York and he wants to hear you play again in his club."

"Well, in that case, I might as well tag along. The show must go on, as the saying goes. You want to come along, Walter?"

Before I could answer, Tim interrupted, looking flustered and embarrassed. "Well, uh, we were going by cab and we won't be able to fit everyone."

"That's all right," said Red. "Walter and I will catch a separate taxi."

Tim's face was flushed. "Look, Red, they only allow certain clientele in the club. They don't allow Negroes."

"Walter's a friend of mine. If he can't go, then I'm not going."

Tim glanced at me, then back at Red. "Hey, look, Red, I don't make the rules. They don't allow colored people in the place, what do you want me to do?"

"Well, like I said, I'm not going."

I was embarrassed and just wanted to get away. I started to remove myself from the bar.
"Don't stay away on account of me, Red," I said. "Go ahead and go. I was heading back to the barracks anyway."

Tim was elated. "You hear that? He doesn't want to go. Come on, Red, they're going to let
us in free, and it's going to be open bar, but that's only if you come."

"I told you already. I'm not going unless Walter comes."

Tim looked at me, then Red, with disgust. He turned and started to walk away, muttering
"Nigger lover" as he went.

Red jumped from his stool. "Better than being an asshole."

Tim turned back around and stormed up to Red. "You calling me an asshole?"

"If the shoe fits," said Red, not backing down. Some of Tim's friends, who were standing at the end of the bar, saw the ruckus and rushed to his side. "You better back off," said Red.

I stood between Tim, his friends, and Red. "Come on guys, settle down, huh? This ain't worth fighting over," I said.

"You're damn right," Tim snarled.

Tim and his friends turned around and started to walk away. Tim turned his head, a look of disgust still on his face, and snarled, "Damn nigger lover." They then walked out of the club. Red and I stood in silence as the rest of the patrons stared at us. We put on our head gear and exited the club. We went outside, apprehensively looking out for Tim and his buddies. They were long gone. We got a six-pack of beer and started to make our way back to the post on foot. We strolled along the dirt road, and an occasional Jeep or army truck passed us. There was a full moon and we were both a little tipsy.

"I appreciate what you did, Red, but you didn't have to do that."

"I wasn't about to let him get away with that racial slur," he said.

"I learned it's best to ignore people like that."

"You mean you weren't insulted?"

"Of course, I was."

Red took a long swig from his bottle."

"I'm white, and that upset me."

"It's best to pay no attention to jerks like that," I repeated. "Besides, it was you and me against how many?"

"I counted six," Red said.

"In that case, it's best to use an old military tactic - retreat and fight another day," I said.

We continued walking in silence until we arrived on post a little after one in the morning. We shook hands and departed to our respective units. I arrived at my barracks to find most of the GI's asleep in their bunk beds. Lloyd, who slept on the top bunk above me, saw me stagger in. He jumped down from the top bunk and assisted me to bed.

"Looks like you really tied one on tonight," he said.

"I only had a few beers."

"How many is a few?"

"About ten," I said.

"You're going to pay for it in the morning. Who were you drinking with?"

"An old friend from New York," I replied.

"You mean that white boy? I'm telling you, Walter, don't get too close to them. You're going to wind up getting stabbed in the back, or worse."

"Mind your own business, Lloyd. Shows how much you know. He stuck up for me against six white guys. It looked like we were going to have a slug-fest, but we managed to get out of it."

"Take my word for it, if you two had fought those white boys, you would have gotten the worst of it."

I paid no attention to Lloyd. As far as I was concerned, Red was a good friend. We promised to meet each other at Toby's after our tour of duty and have a drink of the finest scotch money could buy. I got out of my uniform, folded it neatly in my footlocker, got into bed, and slept, dreaming of Gwen, my mom, dad, and friends in New York City.

CHAPTER 7

We finally received our orders. Lloyd was going to Fort Jackson for infantry training, and I was going to go to Camp Claiborne, Louisiana, for advanced training in tank maneuvers and tactics. I tried to locate Red but found out he had received his orders days earlier and had shipped out for training somewhere in the Midwest. It looked like he'd be fighting in the Pacific theater, against the Japanese. However, most of the military, men, and equipment were scheduled to fight in the Atlantic theater against Germany.

I managed to sneak off post to visit my family and friends. It wasn't hard to do. The trick was getting a ride to the train station. I managed to hitch a ride from an old farmer a couple of miles from base.

I arrived at my mom and dad's apartment. I wanted them to see I was all right and to assure them that my unit would not be shipped overseas. After a meal of oxtails, pigeon peas, and rice, I went over to Toby's to say farewell to friends, and to surprise Gwen. Business was slow when I arrived, as it usually was on a Tuesday. I saw Gwen and Country talking at the other end of the club. She had her cocktail waitress outfit on, showing off her fabulous legs. She looked up and saw me.

"Walter!" she exclaimed. She ran across the room and into my arms. "What are you doing back so soon? I wasn't expecting you for another two months."

"I managed to sneak away. I'm going to Louisiana, and I had to see you before I go."

"I'm working tonight, Walter. But hold on and let me see if Toby will give me the rest of the night off."

"No, don't. I can't stay too long. I have to get back before lights out."

"Well, can you at least stay for one drink?"

"You talked me into it," I said.

"We both laughed as she led me to our special table in the corner.

"You look different, Walter."

"Do I? It must be the haircut."

"No, it's not just the haircut. It's you. You have a different attitude. You're more mature, and your posture is straighter."

"I guess it's all that marching and standing at attention." I chuckled as she looked me over.

Toby strolled up to our table with a cigar in his mouth. He reached into his inside pocket and placed a picture on the table. It was an autographed picture of Billie Holiday. It read, "Good luck to Walter and the boys in your tank unit." I was stunned. I looked at Toby in disbelief.

"Thanks, man! Just like you promised," I said.

I was deeply touched by the gesture from Toby and Billie Holiday, and I told him so. I told him about running into Red and the trouble we had at a night club. The few people who were at Toby's came over to our table and wanted to know about army life. I told them about my experience at the base. I stayed longer than I should have and got back to Fort Upton well after lights out. I was not present for bed count. Lloyd tried to cover for me, but to no avail. I was reprimanded and lost some pay, but it was well worth it.

CHAPTER 8

The train rattled on the narrow tracks on its way to Louisiana. The cars up front were packed with black soldiers. Ten soldiers from my platoon were on the train with me, ready to receive training in tank maneuvers and tactics. It was hot up front, because we were sitting next to the engine. Soot and ashes from the engine blew in through the open window. Embers from the fire flew by one of the guys behind me, and he laughingly hooted and hollered while brushing it off his shoulders. There was joshing, horseplay, and some discreet gambling going on in the middle of the car.

"That's a first," I said to the soldier next to me. "Usually they have us sitting in the rear."

The soldier next to me was reading a book, The Souls of Black Folks, by W. E. B. Du Bois. He wore round rimless glasses and resembled a black owl. "That's because white folks don't want to sit up here next to the engine. It's hot and filled with smoke," he said.

He continued reading his book. I extended my hand. "Hi, I'm Walter Jenkins from New York."

He stopped reading and accepted my hand. "I'm Winston Jones from Detroit. This guy next to me is Tank. He's from Boston."

Tank was a medium-sized, stocky man with huge biceps. He was a little pudgy around the midsection but otherwise seemed to be in good shape. He was admiring the scenery out the train window. He stretched his hand over Winston and shook mine.

"You're not naïve enough to think that we're going to get better treatment than the whites, are you?" he joked. "They don't want to be up here, so they stuck us niggers here." Just then, a sergeant came into the car and ordered us to close the window shutters.

"What for?" one of the soldiers asked.

"Just close them," he snapped.

31

We did what we were told, and all the shutters on the train were drawn. The train pulled slowly through a town. Tank took a quick peek through the curtain.

"Did you see that?" he asked.

"See what?" I asked.

"There were white men out there standing at the station with shotguns and rifles."

Winston momentarily lowered his book.

"Haven't you heard? They were having trouble with these town folks taking pot-shots at cars with Negroes."

"And to think we're going overseas to fight for these crackers," Tank said.

I was going to tell them what that black recruiter had told me, that the brass had no intention of sending us overseas, but I decided against it. It wouldn't do any good telling them, it would only disappoint them. Once the train passed through the town, it slowly picked up speed and continued chugging along the rails.

We arrived at Camp Claiborne in Louisiana, where we were loaded onto army trucks. While we waited, I saw the first signs of the Jim Crow South. There were water fountains with "white only" and "colored only" signs on them. Restrooms, bars, and restaurants were no different. Hearing about it was one thing; actually, witnessing it was another. Being down there in the South, it was a whole other world, a world that I would have to tolerate and get used to.

We loaded onto the army trucks with our duffel bags, about sixteen soldiers on each truck, and were transported to the base. The tarp was drawn down in the back, so we were unaware of where we were going. The trucks climbed hills and made turns, and then about a half-hour later, we came to a halt. Approximately two minutes passed, when suddenly the tarp flew open. Standing outside was a flock of drill sergeants spewing out orders to us to get out of the trucks. There was a bunch of them at each truck, waiting to jump on a recruit.

"Come on, you coons," one drill sergeant yelled. "Grab your duffel bags and move it over there.

Come on, move it, move it!"

One drill sergeant pointed to his right. "Form a formation right over there," he said.

Winston, Tank, and I were the first to form a line. Everyone else went either behind us or beside us. A group of drill sergeants went to the back row and walked up and down the line, picking out the slightest infractions among the men and shouting insults at them. I was standing at attention when a drill sergeant marched up to me.

"Hey, recruit! What's that on your face?" I went to touch my face to inspect it. "Keep your hands down and remain at attention, boy! Did you shave this morning?"

"I didn't get a chance, sir."

Don't call me sir! I'm not an officer, I work for a living. From now on, you refer to me as drill sergeant, understood?"

"Yes, drill sergeant."

The drill sergeant moved his face close to mine. "What's your name, boy?"

"Walter Jen—"

"I don't want to know your first name, recruit," he barked. "What's your last name?"

"Jenkins, drill sergeant."

"Where you from, Jenkins?"

"New York."

"New York?" He moved his face even closer. "Let me tell you something about New York, boy. Nothing but trash comes from New York." I remained at attention, keeping my eyes looking forward, averting eye contact. He stood there for what seemed like an eternity but was probably only a few seconds. "I want to see you clean-shaven before inspection tomorrow, is that clear Jenkins?"

"Yes, drill sergeant."

"I'll be keeping an eye on you."

He moved down the line, hassling other recruits. As I watched him walk down the line, I thought to myself, what am I doing here?

CHAPTER 9

The next few weeks consisted of vigorous training from sunrise to sunset. We did morning pushups, afternoon push-ups, push-ups when we did something wrong, and push-ups just for the hell of it. We went through forced marches, rain or shine. We jogged for miles and did calisthenics. We took apart and reassembled M1 rifles and .45-caliber pistols. There was a soldier in my platoon named Bubba, the son of sharecroppers from Mississippi. He could assemble and reassemble a rifle blindfolded. He helped me along the way, and soon I became proficient.

I had never really learned how to drive a car growing up during the Depression years. My family and I relied on buses, trains and an occasional cab now and then. In boot camp they had to teach me and some of the men how to drive Jeeps, trucks, and motorcycles. I learned how to change oil and clean spark plugs. Once I learned how to drive those vehicles, they started us on tanks. The country boys had no problem maneuvering a tank, being brought up on farms and driving tractors.

Out on the tank range, an instructor would be in the command hatch giving orders and directions. There were two levers on the floor. If you pulled the right lever, the tank turned right; the left lever and it turned left. If you pulled both levers at the same time, the tank would stop. The tank we were training on was an M5 light-weight vehicle, armed with a 37-mm cannon and three .30-caliber machine guns. After weeks of training on the tank, we became good at battlefield tactics and strategy.

One week after another hard day of training, we marched back to our barracks, located at the rear of the base in the lowlands. The white soldiers slept in freshly painted, immaculately clean barracks. The front was spruced up and untarnished. We slept in weather-beaten tents and dilapidated barracks. By the end of the day, I was dog tired from training and flopped on my old bunk. I was lucky in one sense; I got to bunk with some of the guys I had met on the train. Winston sat on his bunk about two rows down from me, reading his book. Tank was naked and ready to take his shower. Bubba was polishing his boots and listening to his radio. Myself, I just lay in my bed, drained and exhausted. The other men were going about their regular routine of playing cards, writing letters, or just horsing around.

"Hey! Can you guys keep it down? I'm trying to read." Winston shouted.

"This ain't no library, man. You want to read, go outside." Tank retorted. He wrapped a towel around his nude body and went to take a shower.

"That must be an interesting book. You've been reading it since you were on the train." I said.

"I'm almost finished. Are you familiar with W. E. B. Du Bois?"

"Of course."

"If you want, when I finish you can read it. It's very enlightening." he said.

"No thanks, I'm a Marcus Garvey man myself."

"Oh, are you?" Winston placed a marker in his book and sat upright. "I can't wait until this training is over, so I can go over there and kill me some of those Kraut bastards."

I was slightly astonished that this seemingly educated man would talk like that. "Why would you want to get involved in this white man's war?"

"Winston adjusted his glasses and looked at me like I had a third eye. "This is not just the white man's war, it's a world war, involving all kinds of nationalities and races."

"The war is mainly in Europe," I argued. "And the last time I checked, it's a white continent."

"What about Africa?" he said. "Rommel and his African Corps are over there right now assisting the Italians in making Africa an Italian empire."

"That's just a small contingent of Hitler's army that's involved. The main battles are taking place in Europe. This is a war that should be fought among white people. It has nothing to do with us."

"It has plenty to do with us. You know what Hitler said about Negroes."

"No different than what the Klan says, and you don't see us marching off to fight them."

"The Klan doesn't have a well-armed army, navy, or air force. W. E. B. Du Bois said that every Negro should take up arms and fight against Nazism, because if Hitler ever wins this war, everything that the black man has achieved will be gone. The slate will be wiped clean."

I looked around the room and saw that everyone was nodding their heads in agreement with

Winston. "How can you go out and risk your life for a country like this?" I asked. "We had to close our shutters on the train to avoid being shot at by those rednecks. German prisoners get treated better than we do, so what are you fighting for?"

"I'm fighting for my country, and race, and to prove to the white man that I can fight."

The men in the barracks began hooting and clapping in agreement with Winston; some walked over and slapped him five. I sat at my bunk bewildered. Not only did the men in this room agree with that sentiment, but most of the men in the battalion did as well. The only reason I was here was because I had been drafted, and the only reason I joined this all-black tank battalion was to make a point to the white establishment that we could handle a tank. I was in full agreement with my father about this being a white man's war. Winston breathed on his glasses, and then wiped the lenses with a piece of tissue. He stood from his bunk and walked over to mine.

"What I don't understand is, if you feel that way about it, then why did you volunteer for this unit?"

"I had no choice, I was drafted."

"This tank unit is all voluntary; more than likely we are going overseas to see some action. If you feel so strongly about it, then why did you volunteer?"

I lay back down on my bunk. I didn't have the heart to tell them that we weren't going overseas to fight. Everyone was training so hard just to prove themselves, to get the opportunity to fight for a country that didn't want them to fight, didn't want them to be part of this great nation. It didn't make sense to me, but it didn't matter. I was just counting the days as they went by, looking forward to going back home and being with Gwen.

CHAPTER 10

One of the most important events that a soldier looked forward to was mail call. It was a little taste of home in all the dust, grime, and smelly swamps. The names of soldier after soldier were called before the drill sergeant finally shouted my name. I double-timed it up to him, and he handed me two letters. One was from my parents and the other was from Gwen. I received mail from them about twice a week. I, in turn, wrote back as often as I could. My mom and dad were doing fine, and Gwen was her usual cheerful self. She wrote that everything was fine and that she's making more money at Toby's due to working more hours. She wrote that she couldn't wait to see me again and that we had a lot of catching up to do.

We got our first weekend pass after four weeks of intense training. Being in the South, riding a bus became a problem for us Negroes. If the bus got too crowded, we would have to sit in the rear. Sometimes, if the bus was overloaded, we would have to get off to make way for the whites. The black soldiers from the South were used to this, but Northern soldiers were not used to that kind of treatment. There was racism where I came from, pretty much everywhere you went. But nothing like this. You couldn't eat here, you couldn't go there. After one month, I was pretty much sick of it. The only place we could go was a small section of town where colored people were allowed. The only problem was how to get there. The white bus drivers were racist and uneducated. And when they wanted you to sit in the back, they told you to do so in a rude and mean-spirited way.

"Hey, boy! Sit in the back," most of them would say. It got to a point that I didn't even want to go to town. I stayed on post with some of the other black soldiers. Winston was one of them. Tank was another. Winston would read and write letters home and went nowhere near town. He finished reading *The Souls of Black Folk* and started his second book by W. E. B. Du Bois, *Black Reconstruction in America*. He offered *The Souls of Black Folk* for me to read, so I accepted - there was nothing better to do. Later that night, Bubba came staggering in. He'd been drinking and was quite drunk. He slept above me on the top bunk.

"I don't know how you guys do it," he said.

His words were slurred from drinking.

"Do what?" I asked.

"Stay here on post day in and day out. You ought to go to the colored section of town, to a place called Mama's House. They serve the best chitlins in Louisiana, and the music is out of sight."

"What type of music?" I asked.

"The blues."

"That's all they play, the blues?"

"That's all."

"I'm a jazz man myself."

"Come on down and listen to the blues. That's Southern music for the black man. I'm going back down tomorrow. You Negroes want to come?"

"I'll go," Tank said.

"What about you, Winston?"

"No, I'll stay here and read."

"What about you, Walter?"

"I don't know. I don't want to have to deal with those bus drivers or white town folks."

"Come on man," said Tank. It's better than being cooped up in here."

The next night I decided to tag along with Bubba and Tank. The ride down wasn't bad, and it was nice getting off post and mingling with the civilians. The food they served was different from what my mom cooked or what I got in the mess hall, but I enjoyed it. They played the blues all night, and I learned to like it. I danced with several women and socialized with a few people. Bubba and Tank came over to the table. Bubba had a bottle of beer in his hand.

"Come on, we got to go," he said. We got to catch the last bus."

I said my goodbyes to the patrons at the table, and the three of us rushed out to catch the bus. We boarded, and the bus was about half full. Most were soldiers from Camp Claiborne. The three of us sat in the middle of the bus, chatting and laughing and having a good time. For the first time in weeks, I was feeling calm and relaxed. There were a few more stops, and the bus was becoming full. The bus driver glanced at the rear-view mirror and ordered us to the rear to make room for some white civilians boarding. Bubba and Tank immediately went to the rear. I remained seated.

"Hey, boy! Didn't you hear me? Get to the back of the bus." He was a chubby man with red cheeks and thick hands. He had a face like a bulldog.

"My name ain't boy. I'm a soldier of the United States Army."

The riders on the bus seemed surprised that I had spoken up and not remain silent. The driver pulled the bus to the side of the road. A whooshing sound came from underneath the bus when he applied the emergency brakes. "You're not going to give me any trouble now, is you boy?"

"I told you before: I'm not a boy. I'm a soldier."

The driver stood up and adjusted his pants over his fat belly. He stared at me for a few seconds. "All right, soldier," he growled. "Get to the back."

I got up from my seat and proceeded to the rear. As I was walking, I saw annoyed and angry white faces looking at me. I don't know what came over me, but I turned and started for the front. "The hell with this. Let me off," I said.

The driver turned the handle and the door flung open. "suit yourself," he snarled.

I stormed off the bus, mumbling a few choice words. The bus sped away with Bubba and Tank looking out the rear window and shaking their heads in disbelief.

It was a long walk back to base. An occasional vehicle passed by, but I dared not ask for a ride. Not in this unfriendly town. It took me a few hours, and I reached base tired and exhausted. I got a ride from a soldier in a Jeep, and he dropped me off at my barracks and sped away. When I went inside, Bubba and Tank were already fast asleep.

***

The next morning, I was in the mess hall with Bubba, Tank, and Winston. There was the sound of dishes and silverware clattering in the background. The cooks were plopping eggs and grits on GIs' plates as they walked down the chow line. I looked at the cooks and thought that this was the job I had contemplated doing before that recruiter talked me into joining a tank battalion.

"I can't believe you did that," said Bubba. "You walked all the way from town."

"I just don't like being treated like that."

Bubba shook his head. "I don't like it either, but that's the way they do things down here."

"That doesn't make it right," said Winston. "W. E. B. Du Bois said that there is no difference between the races. You have intelligent whites and blacks, and some whites and blacks who are not so intelligent. The same goes for all races around the world. The white man gives you that inferiority complex to make himself feel superior."

Bubba put a forkful of scrambled egg mixed with grits into his mouth. "Look, all I'm saying is if you want to survive down here, you got to do what you're told."

"I agree," said Tank "When in Rome, do what the Romans do."

I drank some coffee, then looked at Tank. "How can you say that? I asked. "You're from Boston, one of the most liberal places in America. And you're going to submit to being treated like some sort of farm animal?"

"I don't know about Boston being the most liberal place, and as far as being treated like a farm animal, sitting in the back of the bus don't seem to qualify as that. And what good did it do you? You walked over seven miles to get back to the post." "At least I made my point," I retorted.

"And what point was that? Sore feet and ankles?"

"No, I let that fat cracker know that I wasn't going to put up with that crap."

"Well, I guess you showed him." Bubba quipped.

Winston put some scrambled eggs on his toast and took a huge bite. "Well," he said with a mouthful of food," I have to admire Walter for standing up for his principles. If I was there, I might have done the same thing."

"Principles? What do you black Yankees know about principles? Try living down here, and your precious principles will go straight out the window," Bubba said.

At that moment, five drill sergeants strutted into the mess hall. The lead sergeant was a tall white man with a stern face that looked like it was made out of stone. The other sergeants stood behind him.

"All right, ladies, let's finish up and form a formation outside. Come on, move it!"

CHAPTER 11

Training on the M5 tanks intensified during our final weeks at Camp Claiborne. We were timed on mounting and dismounting. It was tough, but we got better at it as time went by. We marched with full backpacks and set up camp in the woods. One night in the latrine, I had just finished taking my shower when I noticed a bump on my right arm just behind my bicep. Slightly alarmed, I touched the bump to see if there was any pain. There was none. I looked at my left arm to see another bump. I came to realize that those bumps were in fact muscles. I checked my entire body to find that there were muscles on my body I didn't know I had. All the push-ups, jogging, and exercising really paid off.

Although I was in good shape both mentally and physically, problems still persisted in the nearby city of Alexandria. Tension was mounting between white town folk and black soldiers. Military police and bus drivers fared no better. Our commanding officer, Lieutenant Colonel Paul Bates, who was respected by most of the men in the 761st Battalion, could do little to change the feelings of other white officers, or soldiers, or the citizens on Alexandria. But he did forbid any mistreatment of his soldiers. He was the only white officer on the base whom I admired.

I remember in March 1943, near the first anniversary of our battalion, an incident took place in a nearby town. Members of our battalion had been severely beaten by townspeople and police. Tensions were already high when we learned of the death of another black soldier, who had been found cut in half on the railroad tracks. Even though it was ruled that he had been intoxicated, fallen, and passed out on the tracks, he had not been a drinker. When we learned of his death and the ruling, some of the men went down to the motor pool and commandeered several tanks and a half-track. I was standing outside of the motor pool with Winston.

"I'm going with them," Winston said.

"Don't do it, Winston. You don't want to get involved in this." I grabbed his arms and held him back.

"Let go of me!" he shouted.

"Come on, Winston, don't do it. W. E. B. Du Bois never advocated violence. Besides, who's going to help fight the Nazis? Remember what he said - that we should fight Hitler. How are you going to do that when you're dead or in jail? Come on, man. You're too smart for that."

I released Winston's arms, hoping that I had talked some sense into him. Without saying a word, he turned and strolled back to the barracks. The tanks rolled down to the main gate and were met by none other than Lieutenant Colonel Bates. He stopped them at the gate and hopped out of his Jeep.

"You can't do this, men. You're just going to make things worse."

"They can't do this, sir," said one of the tankers. "We've taken enough shit from those people. We're going to drive into town and show them that we can blow their city from the face of the map if we want to."

"This is not the way to go about it. Look, let me go into town and straighten this matter out. And if something like this happens again, I will personally lead you into town myself."

This seemed to placate the men, because they knew as well as I did that when Lieutenant Colonel Bates made a promise, it was written in stone. They returned the tanks to the motor pool and went back to their respective barracks. In the remaining months at Camp Claiborne, the men in our battalion were never again harassed, or bullied by the MP's or the citizens of Alexandria. After that incident, there was no other officer whom I respected more than Bates. I would have laid my life on the line for him. That kind of thinking surprised me.

CHAPTER 12

We arrived at Fort Hood, Texas, for advanced training in tank maneuvers and strategy. Fort Hood was larger than Claiborne, and the training was less strenuous but still intense. We trained on the M4 tank, which was a larger, more powerful version of the M5. It had a V-8 500 horsepower engine and was mounted with a .50-caliber machine gun and a 74-mm cannon. There were two .30-caliber machine guns on each side. Each of us was assigned our own tank. I felt like the tank was my personal property, and my crew and I took pride in our tanks. We made sure they were maintained properly, greasing the wheel bearings and making sure the belts were tightened.

We had some new soldiers come in from Kentucky, and one soldier was assigned to our crew. His name was Bay Bay; he was from my neck of the woods, Harlem, New York. The sergeants picked out the crew members for each tank. My crew consisted of Winston, Bubba, Bay Bay, and me. Winston did well in training, so they made him tank commander; Bubba was the driver, I was the gunner, and Bay Bay, the new man in the group, was the loader.

"So what part of Harlem are you from?" I asked.

"One Hundred Forty-Fifth Street," Bay Bay said.

"You ever been to Toby's?"

His eyes lit up like I was a lost family member.

"You from Harlem, too?" he asked.

"Born and raised."

"I haven't seen a New Yorker since I been here. I've been to Toby's a few times, but the place I mainly hung out at was the Savoy."

We talked a while about New York, Harlem, and the Yankees. Then it came time to name our tanks. That was part of the army tradition. The tanks we trained on in Louisiana were not given names, but the tanks in Fort Hood were our responsibility and we got to name them. Lieutenant Colonel Bates named his tank after his girlfriend, Taffy. Others named their vehicles Thunderbolt, Hurricane, or the Widow Maker.

"What do you want to name our tank?" I asked the crew.

Winston thought for a while.

"How about the Raiders?" he said.

"I like the Black Eagle," Bubba said.

"No, I don't like that," Bay Bay said. "I like the Raiders, but something should be added to it."

"Like what?" I asked.

"Well, seeing that you and I are from Harlem, why don't we call it the Harlem Raiders?"

Everyone seemed to like the name, so we put it to a vote, and all agreed except Bubba, who still wanted to name it the Black Eagle. So it was official, our tank was named the Harlem Raiders. We trained on the tank day and night. We drove at night so we would know how to drive a tank in complete darkness, with nothing but the moon and two pin like lights in the front and back of the tank to guide us. We learned more tank maneuvers and tactics. We trained how to do an orderly advance and retreat. We saw films in the day room on what the Sherman tank could do. We had war games with the white troops, and they would always have us be the Germans. We outmaneuvered them and won almost every battle. Lieutenant General Lear told us in formation that all reports in Washington about us had been of a superior nature.

I was proud of what we'd accomplished. Unfortunately, we were being mistreated by bus drivers, town people, and police in Fort Hood. To my surprise, we were treated worse in the nearby town of Killeen than in Alexandria. The whites in Alexandria would glare at us and shake their heads in dismay. But the local whites in Killeen would shout racial slurs out of their car windows or throw items at us. There was no black side of town where a Negro soldier could go. The nearest place was Austin, which was eighty miles away. So almost all of us remained on base.

The white drivers were intolerable. They would only pick up six black soldiers at a time, and we would have to go directly to the back. White soldiers and civilian employees would board first and come and go as they pleased. When the bus was overloaded, we would have to get off. Some of the bus drivers even carried guns. At the end of the day, the barracks were almost filled to capacity, with most of us spending our free time reading books, writing letters, or just horsing around.

One Saturday afternoon, Winston was lying in his bunk reading yet another book by W. E. B. Du Bois. Bubba was shining his boots, while Bay Bay was writing a letter.

"You know they shipped another white unit out yesterday," Bubba said.

Bay Bay stopped writing his letter and looked up. "Yeah, I heard. They're shipping all those units out and we're stuck here. I don't think we're ever gonna see any fighting."

Winston closed his book and took out some clean tissue to wipe his spectacles. "I heard some white officers say that we aren't anything but black mascots. We're here just to appease the black leadership and voters."

"You guys make it sound like it's a bad thing. We did what was expected, we proved that we can operate and maneuver a tank just as good as any white soldier," I said.

"That's not good enough," said Winston. I want to prove that we can fight just as good."

"Ain't you guys the good little Negroes, willing to die for a country that doesn't give a damn about you," I said.

"I thought we had this discussion already," said Winston. "This has more to do about country. What about pride, and honor?"

"I'm already proud about what we accomplished. White folks thought that we couldn't get this far, what more do you want?"

"To show them that we can go further," Bay Bay interjected. I want more than to say that we trained well, that we can drive a tank. What's the sense of all that knowledge if we can't use it? I can kill a Kraut just as good as anyone else."

Cheers and shouts of "amen" filled the room, and I was the odd man out once again. Nobody agreed with me.

"I'm going out for a cigarette," I said.

I walked into the night air and lit my cigarette. An occasional Jeep or truck passed by. I went for a short walk around the base, trying to clear my head. I thought, am I the only practical one here? Is everyone brainwashed except me? I walked by the Post Exchange and saw German POWs walking around and buying items from the store unattended. Look at this, I thought. The enemy has more freedom than we do. And those fools want to risk their lives for a country like this. I finished my cigarette and walked back to the barracks.

It finally happened, something that had been long overdue. A soldier disobeyed a bus driver's orders to sit in the back of the bus. Jackie Robinson, a lieutenant who later became the first black Major League Baseball player, refused to sit in the rear. It caused a fire storm of controversy. The army was forced to acknowledge that there was a problem with segregated buses. Through public pressure, the army decided to make it public policy that there would be no segregated buses on post. The bus driver either knew or had chosen not to honor it. Angry words were expressed between Robinson and the driver. Robinson was escorted to the military police station, where more angry and racial words were expressed. We were out on maneuvers when all this occurred.

When we returned from the field, it was a subject that everybody was talking about. We later learned that there would be a court-martial of Lieutenant Robinson.

I was sitting at a table in the mess hall with Bubba, eating a meal of corned beef hash and potatoes. "That's no way to treat an officer of the US military," I said.

"He should have just sat in the back and avoided all this hassle," Bubba said.

"You may not be aware of this, Bubba, but there's a new regulation that says that as long as we're on post, we don't have to sit in the back of the bus."

Bubba drank some water from his glass, and then laughed. "I'm from Mississippi, so I should know. I don't care what kind of regulation the army comes up with; this is the South, and old traditions die hard. I heard that Robinson cursed at the bus driver. A white man, at that. You don't do that sort of thing down here. Now he's gonna be court-martialed and get a dishonorable discharge, his military career ruined. Now, I myself don't think it was worth it. All he had to do was just sit in the back."

"I don't care about the South or its traditions," I said. "As long as that new regulation exists, and

I'm on post, I'm going to sit anywhere I please. And if any of those crackers tell me to sit in the back, I'm gonna tell them where they can go."

Bubba let out another laugh. "I know you will," he said.

"It sure beats walking seven miles," I said. We both laughed.

CHAPTER 13

I first met Charles Walton sometime late in August. I did not know at the time that meeting this man would change my outlook on life. He was medium built, slim, and wore a part in the middle of his hair. He had smooth skin and a baby face with a fuzzy mustache. He was with the 458th, another black tank battalion, which was attached to us. They drove lightweight tanks mounted with smaller cannons and two .30-caliber machine guns. They were used most of the time for reconnaissance and light fighting. He was watering down the tank when I saw him.

"How fast does that tank go?" I asked.

"It can go up to forty or fifty miles," he said.

I whistled in amazement.

"That fast, huh?"

"Yeah, it's not meant to do heavy fighting, just go in and out as fast as we can without being detected."

"I sure would hate to go up against a German Panzer in that," I said.

"I would hate to go up against a Panzer in anything," he answered. He got some soapy water and started washing down the other side of the tank.

"So, where you from?" I asked.

"Iowa."

"Iowa? They have Negroes living in Iowa?"

"Yeah. Not a large population, but there's a few of us there. Where you from?"

"New York."

"Oh yeah? What part?"

"Harlem."

"You're from Harlem? I heard a lot about Harlem. I always wanted to visit, never got a chance."

"Maybe if we pass through there, I'll show you around."

"I would like that."

He finished soaping down the side of the tank and began watering it down with the hose. I went over to the mess hall for lunch, then went about my daily duties. Mail call was at four o' clock in the day room. I got my usual mail from my mom and dad and Gwen. I hadn't received a letter from Gwen for about two weeks and was happy to see that she had finally found time to write me. My father wrote that he was getting more hours and making more money at the docks. My mother got a part-time job as a housekeeper in Queens. I was happy to hear that my folks were making a little more money. I was going to send them some, but it looked like they didn't need it.

I finally opened Gwen's letter. My heart sank when I read the first sentence: "Dearest Walter, I didn't plan for this to happen, it just happened. I tried to stay true to you but certain circumstances happened beyond my control."

I couldn't believe what I was reading. She had left me for another guy. She didn't say who, she just said that she knew that she told me she would wait, but couldn't. She ended the letter by saying

"Sincerely yours," not even "with love."

Disappointed, I went through the rest of the day in a slump. I didn't speak much to anyone. I walked around in a daze. Gwen was my inspiration, the reason why I got up in the morning to do my daily routine, to want to be one of the best tankers in the army. She inspired me. Now the desire to finish up my years of duty and get married was gone. I had some money saved to buy her an engagement ring. After duty hours, I got some of that money and went to the PX. I got myself a bottle of whiskey and went to a wooded area. I sat on a boulder and read the letter once more. I took a long pull from the bottle. How she could do this? I thought. We had so much going for us. I

wiped a tear from my eye and took another swig from the bottle.

An army Jeep passed, then slowed and went in reverse to where I was sitting. There were two MPs in the vehicle. The one on the passenger side shone a flashlight on me. "You're not drinking over there, are you, soldier?" he asked. "I'm just having a few. I'm off duty."

The two MPs exited the vehicle.

"It doesn't matter," he said. "You know you're not supposed to be drinking out in the open on government property. You can drink in the enlisted men's club or in the barracks, but not out here."

The other MP noticed the letter in my hand. "Bad news from home?" I nodded my head. He took my bottle and emptied the remaining contents on the ground. "I'm going to let you slide this time. Next time you won't be so lucky. Why don't you head back to your barracks and sleep it off?"

I got up and staggered back to my barracks, feeling lucky that they didn't push the issue. The next morning, I felt worse than the day before. I was hung over, and the pain of Gwen's leaving me was even more intense. It was Saturday, an off-duty day. No one was in the barracks but me. I looked at my watch and saw that it was eight thirty. Damn! I thought. I missed breakfast. I went into my footlocker and retrieved two aspirins. I washed them down with a glass of water. Tank came strolling in from outside.

"You're finally up," he said.

"Why didn't somebody wake me?"

"We tried. You were really out of it."

I wet a towel, lay down on my bunk, and placed the wet towel across my forehead.

"Have you heard?" he asked.

"Heard what?"

"There's a rumor going around that we're going to be shipped out."

"Shipped out where?"

"Don't know. Either the Pacific or over to Europe."

"That's just what it is, a rumor," I said.

Tank looked around to make sure no one was listening, and then he moved closer to me and lowered his voice. "I know the clerk over at headquarters, and he said that Major Wingo is part of an advanced detachment sent to bases to prepare us for departure overseas." Major Wingo was second in command with the 761st, and not happy to be attached with us. The feeling was mutual with most of us in the 761st.

"What base?" I asked.

"I don't know."

"He's probably preparing our departure for a base here in the States. We're not going overseas," I said.

"What makes you so sure?"

50

The aspirin was kicking in and my headache was beginning to fade. "Look, this is between you and me, but my recruiter assured me that we're not going into combat."

"That don't mean nothin'," said Tank. "My recruiter told me we wouldn't be doing much walking because we'll be riding tanks, and as you know, that's bull."

I lay back on my bunk and placed the towel back on my head. "Believe what you want, Tank. But we're not going anywhere."

CHAPTER 14

It turned out that Tank was right. On Monday morning we received an alert for deployment. This meant that we were going to either the Pacific to fight the Japanese or Europe to fight the Germans. My knees suddenly felt weak when I received the news, and I stood there dazed in disbelief. All this time I had thought they would never send us overseas to fight. I thought that all I had to do was train hard to prove to everyone that we could be a fighting unit. The irony was that we did so well in training that General George Patton asked for us himself. Most of the men in the 761st Battalion welcomed the opportunity to prove themselves in battle. Myself, I was disappointed. It turned out not to be a good month for me. First Gwen left me, then I got the news that I was going into combat. I really needed Gwen's companionship, someone to hold and talk to before I deployed.

On August 9, 1944, we boarded the US troop train at Camp Hood. We had no idea where we were going. Everything was kept secret. We even had to take off our unit patches so enemy spies wouldn't know our movements. As the train rattled down the tracks, the soldiers were enthusiastic about their future endeavors, excited about finally getting a chance to prove themselves. Several MP's walked through the troop cars, pulling down the shades.

"Why are you pulling down the shades?" one of the soldiers asked.

"It's for your own protection," the MP answered.

For our own protection? I thought. We're being sent to fight for these hillbillies and they're taking pot-shots at us. And these soldiers, the guys I'm with, are willing to fight for them. They seem oblivious to the fact that war is an abomination.

I had spoken with several veterans from World War I, both black and white, and they relayed to me in great detail how ugly war can be. It's not like in the movies, the veterans told me. You don't get shot and die peacefully. It's messy. You wither and suffer in pain, hoping someone will reach you in time. You get your arms and legs blown off. One minute you're talking and laughing, and the next you're headless. You never know when you're going to buy the farm. I lit a cigarette and was tempted to peek out the window but dared not to in fear of getting shot. I sure was glad to be getting out of the South. Bubba walked up the aisle and stooped down next to us. "I managed to get a look outside," he said. "And we're heading northeast."

"Are you sure?" Winston asked.

"Positive."

"All right!" exclaimed Tank. "I'll be shooting some Krauts."

"You know, Tank, they have bullets too, and they'll be shooting right back," I said. "And I'll be waiting with my seventy-four-millimeter cannon to fire back on their asses."

"This ain't no game. This is real life and death, blood and guts," I said.

"You know," Winston intervened, "we're not in the mood to listen to your cynical views right now."

CHAPTER 15

Three days after our departure from Fort Hood, we arrived at Camp Shanks, in Orangeburg, New York. Thousands of soldiers passed through every day. It was a staging point for the European theater. We were staying there for a few weeks to get inoculations and do paperwork. We were scheduled to leave in three weeks to a month. A group of us got overnight passes, and we decided to catch the train across the George Washington Bridge to Harlem. Charles from the 458th Tank Battalion tagged along with me, Bubba, Winston, and Bay Bay. Tank could only stay with us a little while; he was going to catch a bus to Boston. After Tank's bus departed, we hopped in a cab and were on our way to my parents' apartment.

"You sure your folks won't mind having all us niggers there?" Bubba joked.

"They're looking forward to meeting you guys. When was the last time you had a home cooked meal?" I asked.

"Man, it's been too long," Bubba was looking out the cab window and was amazed at the big city. "This sure ain't nothing like Mississippi," he said.

"So, what will your mother be serving?" Winston asked.

"Curried goat."

"Curried what?"

"Curried goat. It's a Jamaican dish."

"When you say goat, do you mean an actual goat?"

"Yeah, what else would it be?"

"I'm not eating no goat," Bubba said.

I looked at Bubba and laughed. "Bubba, you'll eat just about any part of a pig. You'll eat pig ears, legs, feet, guts, brains, and you're afraid of a little goat?"

"I'm not eating no goat," he repeated.

We arrived at my parents' place and were greeted at the door by my mother and father. I introduced them to my friends, then all six of us sat at the table. My father dished out rice, vegetables, and curried goat. To my surprise, Bubba had two helpings.

"I was kind of hesitant at first," he said, "but this goat ain't bad."

We all had a good time with my parents. We talked and laughed, and if my folks still had reservations about me going to Europe, they didn't show it. After dinner, we decided to go to the legendary Savoy. We went outside and tried to hail a cab.

"Hey, look fellows," I said. Before we go to the Savoy, there's a club I want to go to first. It's not far from here, it's within walking distance." They agreed and we walked over to Toby's. I really wanted to see Gwen. Maybe if I could talk to her, see her again, she might change her mind. The four of us walked over to Toby's and were greeted at the door by Toby himself. His eyes widened when he saw me standing at the doorway. He stretched out his hand and we shook.

"My man, Walter! I see you brought some of your army buddies with you," he said.

I introduced Toby to my friends, and he led us to a table in the corner, the same table that Gwen and I used to sit at. It was a packed house, with other soldiers and sailors among the crowd. We sat at the table and ordered drinks. Fats Waller was on stage, playing the piano with his band. Bubba and Bay Bay got up from the table and found two women to dance with. I scanned the club hoping to spot Gwen, but there was no sign of her. Charles was nursing his beer.

"So how do you like New York so far?" I asked.

"Charles looked up from his drink and smiled. "It's all right, I guess."

"You haven't said ten words since we got here."

"Don't mind me, I'm a little shy sometimes," he said.

"Loosen up, man, we're in the Big Apple. Enjoy yourself."

I noticed a woman standing in front of the bar with some friends, looking at Charles. "Hey,

Charles, I think those ladies at the bar are checking you out."

"They're not my type," he said.

"Not your type? Don't be silly, man. Get up there and dance with one of them."

Charles just sat there nursing his beer. "Naw, maybe later."

Toby came over to our table with a woman whose hand was clasped around his arm. He had a cigar clenched to the side of his mouth.

"Having a good time, Walter?" he asked.

"Yeah. I've been gone a couple of months, but somehow it seems longer. Is Gwen working tonight?"

Toby looked at me, then whispered something in the woman's ear. She turned around and headed for the bar.

"Can I talk to you, Walter?" Charles got the hint and excused himself from the table. Toby pulled out a chair and sat down, looking at me with concern. "I hate to be the one to tell you this, but Gwen is seeing someone else."

"I know. She wrote me a letter a couple of weeks ago."

"You know? And you still want to see her?"

"I love her," I said. We were planning on getting married when I got out."

Toby took a drag on his cigar. "I'm only telling you this, Walter, because I like you, but Gwen is not the type of woman you can depend on."

"What are you trying to say?"

Toby took another drag on his cigar. He looked at me, then shook his head. "I said enough already." He pushed his chair from the table and was about to stand.

"Come on, Toby, you got something to say, why don't you just spit it out?"

Toby pulled his chair back to the table. "Gwen's the kind of girl that won't wait for anybody.

She's what you call a free spirit."

"I don't care what you say. I'm going to get her back, even if I have to fight for her."

"Listen to me, Walter. I'm older than you and I know women. She's not worth fighting for."

"Why don't you mind your own business and let me decide whether she's worth fighting for or not." I was starting to get annoyed with him.

"She was seeing other men behind your back, before you went in the army," Toby said abruptly.

"What?"

"I'm telling you Walter, she's not worth it."

"Who's she with now?" I asked.

Toby hesitated and took another drag on his cigar. I was furious. The girl I loved and planned to marry was double-timing me while we were dating. "Come on, Toby, tell me," I said.

"It was Country."

"Country?" I shook my head in shock. "Country?" I repeated.

"She's with him right now in some cabin in the mountains."

"She was with Country all this time, even when we were dating?"

"I'm sorry, Walter. There are plenty of women out there. You're a nice-looking guy, you shouldn't have trouble finding somebody else."

"You don't understand," I said in a whisper. "She was the one, the only one."

"Wait a minute," said Toby. "Were you a virgin? Was Gwen your first?"

I nodded my head. Toby started laughing. "Come on, man," he said. "Snap out of it and take my advice. Date other women, and I guarantee, in a couple of weeks, you'll forget all about her."

I was sad, disgusted, and angry. I was angry at Gwen for betraying me, angry at Country for stabbing me in the back, and angry at Toby for not telling me sooner. The woman who was with Toby returned with a drink.

"Well, I guess I have to go. Business calls. I'll talk to you later, Walter." Toby got up from the table and he and the woman went to the bar. I remained seated, thinking about Gwen and Country. I remembered that every time I walked in the club, they would be engaged in conversation. And I thought nothing of it. How could I be so stupid? I had thoughts of confronting Country, but who was I kidding? Country used to box in the streets, and he was a good boxer at that. There were rumors that he used to spar with Joe Louis. I even heard he fought six cops at the same time in Louisiana. Although I had taken up some boxing, I wouldn't stand a chance against him. He would mop the floor with me. Charles returned to the table with a fresh beer.

"Everything okay?" he asked.

"Fine," I replied.

A chubby woman walked up to our table. "Hello, soldier," she cooed. She had a wide gap between her front teeth. We both said hi, and she pointed towards the bar.

"You see those two girls standing over there?" Charles and I looked up and saw two fairly attractive women at the bar flirting with us. "Well," she continued, "they would like it if you two would come over and buy them a drink."

"Not now for me. How about you, Charles?" Charles shook his head. "I'll tell you what," I said.

"I'll buy all three of you a drink. Tell the bartender to put it on my tab."

"You're not coming over?" she asked disappointed.

"My friend and I are not in the mood right now." As the woman walked back to the bar, I took another pull from my glass. Charles gazed at me.

"You know, you could've gone over there if you wanted to. You didn't have to stay on my account."

"Nah, I don't feel like socializing with women right now."

"Did you have a bad breakup?" he asked.

"Yeah, a girl I was going to marry."

"I just recently had a breakup myself," Charles said.

We clicked our glasses and swore an allegiance against women.

We left Toby's around ten and headed for the Savoy. We heard Duke Ellington was playing there, and we didn't want to miss him. Bubba and Winston managed to couple up with two women from Toby's. We caught two cabs and managed to squeeze all seven of us in. We arrived at the club around half past ten, and I was amazed at the crowd that was there. Bubba had never seen anything like it, being from the South. Bubba and Winston went instantly to the dance floor with their dates and joined the other party goers. They were doing the jitterbug on the famous Savoy hardwood floor. Bay Bay went around trying to find a dance partner. Charles and I had no intention of dancing with anyone. We both ordered drinks at the bar.

"So, how long has it been since you broke up with your girlfriend?" I asked.

"Just before I joined the army," Charles said.

"At least you knew about it before you went in. My girlfriend broke up with me during my training." We drank and talked some more about our ex-girlfriends. I noticed that he seemed to be more open with me than he was with the other men.

CHAPTER 16

W e had our heavy barracks bags as we boarded the Esperance Bay, a rickety ship that had been constructed in London. We were bound for England, then to France to fight the war in Europe. As usual, the ship was segregated, with the colored troops quartered at the bottom of the boat, while the white troops rode in the bow and the mid-ship areas. Most of us stayed in our respective areas and did not journey around the ship much. Tank lost some weight due to sea sickness; he couldn't keep most of his food down. I felt a little queasy but did not get fully sick. Most of us had never been on a ship that size before, and we were in awe of its size and beauty. It was tough being cooped up down below, but we managed to cope. We reached Avon mouth, England, on September 8, 1944, after spending eleven days at sea. Although Tank had lost some weight, he seemed healthier. His pot belly was almost gone. When we docked and unloaded from the ship, we could not help but notice the uniqueness of England compared to the United States.

The buses had two decks and were painted red. The policemen did not carry guns and wore bobby hats. We boarded a train that took us to a small town called Wimborne, about twenty miles from the southern coast of England. They had us stay in barns and outbuildings. After we unpacked our gear and were briefed, we settled in to await further orders. In a few days, we were given passes. In morning formation, a Southern white captain stood in front of us.

"So, you men are going to be issued passes. I want you boys to remember one thing: you are representatives of the United States of America, so carry yourselves accordingly." He shook his head. "I don't believe I'm doing this," he said, "signing passes for black soldiers to carry on with white women. My grandmother would spin in her grave if she ever knew."

One of the soldiers in the background shouted, "Spin, granny, spin!"

Bubba, Winston, Bay Bay, Tank, and I were ready to go off post and into town to visit the local pubs. We had our dress uniforms on and were ready to depart, when Winston stopped us at the door.

"Wait a minute, you guys. Over at the town hall just down the road a piece, there's a welcoming committee waiting for us. Why don't we stop off there before we go into town?"

"A welcoming committee?" Tank asked. "Are there going to be booze and broads there?"

"Nothing like that. It's going to be housewives and English veterans welcoming us to England," Winston said.

"What kind of refreshments are they going to serve?" I asked.

"It's not going to be liquor. They'll be serving coffee, tea, and cookies."

"We don't have time for that," Bubba said. "Let's go into town."

"Come on, you guys, they went through all this trouble to set it up for us. The least we can do is stop over for a little while. We have plenty of time to go into town," Winston said.

The five of us went to the town hall not far from the post. We walked inside a large room to find other Negro soldiers from around the area, conversing and drinking tea and eating crumpets. There were balloons hanging around the room and a large banner on the wall that read, "Welcome to England, Negro American Soldiers." There was a short line of people waiting to be served. I waited in line and received a cup of tea and some type of cookie. I was served by an attractive middle-aged, English woman.

"Welcome to England, and God bless," she said in her thick British accent.

After receiving my tea and cookies, I scanned the room to see if I could locate Winston and the rest of my group. They were sitting on the floor next to an elderly man in an armchair. He was in his eighties, maybe older, and he was having a conversation with them. They were sitting next to an open flame at the fireplace. The fire was burning evenly, and everyone seemed snug and comfortable. The elderly man had white hair and a white beard. He looked like a skinny Santa Clause. He wore a Scottish kilt, revealing his ashy white legs. I strolled up to them, and everyone turned their attention to me.

"You're just in time," Bay Bay said excitedly. "He's just about to tell us the battle he had with the Zulus." I was quite intrigued. History had been my favorite subject in high school.

"You were in the Zulu war?" I asked.

"Yes, I was, mate," he said in a feeble voice. "Why don't you grab a seat and I'll tell you about it." I instantly sat down, excited to be listening to an actual soldier who had fought in the Zulu war.

"Well, there I was," he said, "me mates right next to me. We were looking at the hill in front of us, waiting. And there they were, hundreds of them, with spears and shields chanting some ungodly words and clapping their hands in some sort of ritual. Well, those savages pointed their spears and held up their shields, then charged at us. Waves of those bloody black heathens came toward us, and I waited to hear the command from me captain to fire, but there was none. When those black devils were almost upon us, the order was given and we fired on them. We must have—"

"Wait a minute," Winston interrupted. "You left your country to invade another and you're making yourself seem justified in killing those people." The old man was taken aback by Winston's outburst.

"Well it was part of our country," the old man said.

"Since when is Africa a part of your country? Or India, or Ireland, for that matter."

"It's part of the British Empire."

"All those 'black devils,' as you like to call them, were doing was defending their land."

The old man's face flushed with embarrassment. "I didn't mean to insinuate –" he stumbled over his words. "Those were Africans, not Americans," he said.

"Those Africans are part of us. They're our ancestors."

I stood up to try to take control of the situation. "Calm down, will you, Winston? This is all part of history."

"It's not the part that I'm proud of, and you Uncle Toms sit there starry-eyed while he tells stories of hundreds of blacks being slaughtered."

The old man slowly stood from the armchair. "Maybe it's best that I go. I didn't mean to insult you, young fellow." He gingerly walked away as Bubba, Tank, Bay Bay, and I looked at Winston, dumbfounded. The people in the room fell silent and were looking at us. One by one, we stood up and walked out. Winston was in front of us. When we got outside, I rushed up to him, blocking his path.

"What's the matter with you, Winston? The man is telling an interesting story, a part of history, and you had to go make a scene."

"I'm not going to stand around while he belittles my people."

"Your people? They're Africans," Bubba said.

"And those Africans are part of our culture. Marcus Garvey once said that Africa is in us all."

"What is it with you, Winston?" I asked. "Must everything always be black and white with you?

Can't you just enjoy one evening without injecting politics into it?"

"Don't tell me about politics, if you-"

"Hey! Come on, guys," Tank interjected. "We're here to have a good time, not fight among ourselves. Come on, let's go into town and have a good time."

Bubba grabbed Winston's collar. "I don't appreciate you calling me an Uncle Tom."

"Take it easy, man. I was just trying to make a point." Winston said.

"Let go of him, Bubba," Tank said.

Bubba glared at Winston for a few seconds before releasing him.

CHAPTER 17

We walked along the English streets admiring the view of grand old England. There were a few bombed out sites, where Tank took pictures. Bubba noticed Charles coming out of a building with a blond man. He saw us and quickly rushed the man off. We all walked up to him.

"Hey, Charles, how you doing?" I asked.

Charles extended his hand and we all shook. "So, what are you guys doing around here?" he asked.

"We're just hanging out, trying to find one of those famous English pubs," Winston said.

"Is that a pub? I asked, looking at the building Charles and the man had just left. On the door was a sign that read, "Ole Brothers Place."

"Yes, it is, but there's nothing happening in there," Charles said.

"Well, let's go check it out," Winston said.

Charles blocked Winston from going inside. He pointed down the street to another building. "There's a nice pub right there," he said.

I could hear jazz music coming from the building, so we all walked over. "Hey, they're playing my kind of music," I said. "Come on, let's go inside."

We all went inside and discovered a sea of white faces staring at us. There were white soldiers and some locals dancing and drinking. The jukebox was playing music from the Andrew sisters, and the soldiers were dancing with some English women. I didn't see one black face. I immediately began getting bad vibes."

"You know, maybe we'd better go," I said.

Winston looked at me, surprised. He adjusted his glasses and walked in front of me. "Why do you want to go? We have every right to be here."

"I'm getting a bad feeling about this place," I said.

"You forget," Winton said, "we're in England. This isn't Alabama, and I don't see any sign that says, 'whites only.'"

Winston strolled inside with Bubba, Tank, Bay Bay, and Charles behind him. I stayed at the door, but reluctantly followed them. Winston strolled up to the bar. There was a tall, beefy, blond soldier sitting on a stool. A wooden dance floor was on the right side. White soldiers were dancing with the local women, who seemed to be enjoying themselves. They were now dancing to a Duke Ellington tune, "It Don't Mean a Thing If It Ain't Got That Swing."

Straight ahead was the bar, with a mirror in the background and neatly stacked glasses. The bartender was a short, dark haired man with a round face and reddish cheeks. The blond soldier had a glass of beer in front of him. Next to him was a dark-haired soldier whose hair was thinning at the top. He had a mustache similar to Clark Gable's. The music was still blaring, but the patrons on the dance floor stopped dancing. I could feel eyes digging into me like little daggers. The bartender was wiping down a glass and seemed unaware of the tension in the room.

"What will you have, mates?"

"We'll have three beers and one whiskey," Winston said. "What will you have, Charles?"

Charles nervously looked around the tavern. "I'll have a whiskey."

"What about you Walter?"

It was a cool night, but I felt sweat dripping from my forehead. I wanted to have a relaxing evening, to see the sights and dance, to try to forget about Gwen. I didn't want this, to be around people who looked down on us like we were a curse, a nightmare. We wear the same uniform, we're fighting the same enemy, but we're not eligible to be in the same room.

"I'll have bourbon," I said.

"All right, bartender, we'll have three beers, two whiskeys, and one bourbon."

The bartender hurried off to get the drinks. The blond soldier sipped his beer and looked at us menacingly. "You know, there's a pub not far from here where there's plenty of your kind," he said.

Winston took off his glasses and placed them in his top pocket.

"I kind of like this place," he said.

"You're not wanted here. Why don't you boys just leave."

"I have every right to be here. Look around, big fella, this is England. There's no Jim Crow law here. If you don't like our company, why don't you go?"

The big blond soldier sprang from his stool. "We were here first."

"I don't care if you were here first, you have two choices. You can stay or you can leave. It's up to you."

The blond soldier continued looking down on Winston. He was a big fellow, about six foot four. He was about to say something, but I interrupted.

"Why don't we just leave, Winston?"

"If you want to leave, Walter, go ahead. I'm staying."

"Why don't you listen to your friend and skedaddle," said the blond soldier. "Unless you're looking for trouble."

At that moment, the bartender returned with our drinks. The people on the dance floor resumed dancing, and the folks in the pub continued conversing with one another. But there was still tension around the bar area. The bartender placed the drinks on the counter. Realizing the uneasiness at the bar, he attempted to quell the hostility with some humor.

"You know, we British have a saying about you Yanks," he said.

The blond soldier turned his attention from Winston to the bartender. "Yeah, what's that?"

"You're overpaid, oversexed, and over here."

"Oh yeah," said the blond soldier. "Well, you Brits are underpaid, undersexed, and under Eisenhower."

Everyone at the bar laughed as the bartender hurried off into the back room. For a brief moment, the hostility seemed to have melted away. Bubba and the rest of us laughed at the blond soldier's humorous comeback. The white soldiers at the bar laughed along with us, and we all chuckled and roared in unison. As suddenly as it started, it ended, the blond soldier's laugh turned into a frown, and the anxiety returned.

"Now, are you boys leaving or what?" he said.

"Man, you are persistent," Winston replied.

The blond soldier finished the rest of his beer and slammed the empty glass on the counter. "I'm afraid I'm going to have to insist," he said. "This here is a private party, and you're not invited."

"This is a public place, and as long as I'm a guest of this country, I have every right to be here."

The dark-haired soldier took the blond soldier by the elbow. "Come on, forget about it, Ben. It's not worth the hassle."

"No! I'm not drinking with any niggers!"

The tension at the bar was unbearable with apprehension. I looked around the pub trying to think of some kind of strategy. The jukebox started playing a Billie Holiday tune, "Them Their Eyes." Not intimidated, Winston coolly looked Ben in the eyes.

"Well, you can leave."

Ben snatched Winston's arm and pulled it. "You're getting out of here if I have to throw you out myself."

Winston threw a punch into Ben's mouth. Ben shook it off, picked him up like a rag doll, and tossed him into the mirrored wall behind the bar. Bubba lunged forward and threw an overhand right punch to Ben's jaw. He staggered backwards, knocking over some chairs. The dark-haired soldier jumped on Bubba's back. Tank punched a white soldier in the face. There was sudden mayhem in the bar. Tables were smashed, chairs were thrown. The patrons on the dance floor stopped dancing. Some joined the fight, others watched. Women were screaming and trying to exit the premises. It was utter chaos.

A fist hit my stomach, another just above my right eye. I spun and whacked somebody with my forearm. A white soldier tried to hit Bubba with a chair. Bubba moved to his side, avoiding it, and hit the soldier three times. His fist was like a blur. A soldier took a swing at me. I ducked and he barely missed, exposing his left side. I gave him two quick jabs that sent him to the floor. Another soldier tackled me. He managed to get on top of me, but before he could throw any punches, Tank grabbed him from behind and tossed him aside. I sprang to my feet and began punching at anything that moved. I hit one soldier with a right cross, another with two left jabs. Those boxing lessons really paid off.

I hit another soldier with a left hook, and then a right cross. He came back with a left jab that caught me off guard; I guess he had taken boxing lessons too. I threw two left jabs at him, and he came back with a right cross that rang my bell. I was dazed for a second or two, giving him time to pick up a chair to swing at me. I managed to refocus in time to avoid the chair. I swung at him with a right cross, missing him and losing my balance and falling into the arms of a white soldier behind me. He grabbed me and held on. I tried to break away, but his grip was too strong. The other soldier hit me in the mid-section with a right, then a left.

Out of the corner of my eye, I saw Charles fighting with lightning speed. He jumped in the air, placing a kick squarely in a soldier's face. He spun around and caught another soldier in the jaw. They both went down to the floor. He spotted me in trouble and darted across the room. He planted his right foot and spun around, blindsiding the soldier punching me. He yelled for me to duck. I bent my head and he gave the soldier holding me a straight forward punch. The soldier backed away, blood spurting from his broken nose. Someone hit Charles from behind. He turned around and began battling with that person. Someone tackled me, and I was on the floor tussling with him. It looked like we were about to be overwhelmed, when we heard the shrill of whistles blaring through the air. Local police and MPs were entering the establishment, blocking people from leaving.

"Quick! This way!" Charles shouted.

We ran down the corridor leading to another exit, where four black MPs stood. "Where do you guys think you're going?"

CHAPTER 18

Captain Fitzgerald was the watch commander. He had bright-red hair and freckles, similar to my friend Red, with a pointed nose and chin. His office was large by army standards, with seven green file cabinets side by side in a corner. A green desk was opposite from the door, and a conference table was in the middle of the room. There were seven straight chairs and a window overlooking the main road. Tanks could be heard rattling by the window as well as the occasional sound of a sergeant shouting cadence to his marching soldiers. There was a photo on his desk of a woman with a pink dress. Charles, me, Ben, and his white buddies were led into the room by four MPs. We had just spent the night in the stockade, and the MPs were ordered to bring us into Captain Fitzgerald's office. One of the MPs gave the captain papers to sign. He signed them, and then the MP saluted and left the room with the others, leaving us standing at attention in front of the captain who, I might add, was not happy to see us. We were a sorry looking lot. Ben's left eye was swollen and almost shut; his shirt was torn and blood-stained. The guy next to him had a busted lip and ripped shirt. I had swollen lips and a puffed-up face. The only one who was unscathed was Charles.

With the exception of some ripped buttons on his shirt, he did not appear to have been in a fight. Captain Fitzgerald shook his head in disgust as he looked at us.

"Look at you guys. I have never seen a sorrier bunch of sad sacks. You call yourselves soldiers?" he said. He walked behind his desk, still shaking his head. He opened his desk drawer and withdrew a pouch. He took out some tobacco, neatly pressed it into his pipe, and lit it evenly. He blew out some smoke and observed the five of us standing in front of him. He walked in a straight line, glancing at each of us. "What are you guys trying to do, start a race riot here in England?" Ben started to answer. "Sir, they came crashing into our private party—"

Before he could finish, Captain Fitzgerald marched up to him, his face inches away. "I don't believe I gave you permission to speak, private!" he shouted. "If I want an explanation, I'll ask for it." He resumed walking in front of us. You men are supposed to be representing the United States of America, and this is how you represent us? By acting like a bunch of hooligans in a local tavern?" We remained silent as the captain glanced at each of us. He took a drag on his pipe, and then sat behind his desk. "All right, private, you wanted to speak. What do you have to say for yourself?"

Ben remained at attention and kept his eyes forward. He cleared his throat. "Well, sir, we were having a private party at the pub when these two guys and their friends came waltzing in. We tried to explain to them that it was a private party, but they refused to leave."

"Did the owner agree for you to have a private party in his saloon?"

"We mentioned it to him."

The captain stood in front of his desk. "I said, did the owner agree for you to have a private party? Did he agree to it or not?" He stared sternly at Ben. "You had better be truthful, because I'm going to question the owner about this later."

Ben shuffled his feet nervously.

"I'm going to take that as a no," Captain Fitzgerald said. "So, you decided to have a private party without the owner's consent."

"Sir, there was a pub about four blocks down the street. There was plenty of colored there that they could have mingled with."

"So now were getting to the crux of the matter. You didn't want them there because they were colored."

Ben remained silent, his eyes fixed straight ahead.

"What's your last name, private?"

"O'Brian, sir."

"O'Brian? So, you're Irish, like me. I don't know if you're old enough to remember the days when merchants and businesses would hang signs on their windows stating that Irish need not apply." The captain walked up to the dark-haired soldier.

"And you're Private Seymour, right?"

"Yes, sir."

"You're Jewish, right?" Seymour nodded. "I can't begin to tell you the atrocities that are taking place over in Germany."

Seymour hung his head. Captain Fitzgerald pointed to the other soldier next to Seymour. "And you, what's your name, soldier?"

"Grasso, sir."

"That's Italian, isn't it?"

"Yes, sir."

"The welcome mat wasn't exactly rolled out for your kind either."

The captain returned to his desk and took another drag on his pipe. He observed each of us. "What I'm trying to say, gentlemen, is that we all came to America in different ships, but we're all in the same boat. We're here in this country as Americans, from all types of backgrounds, fighting against Nazism, the cancer that is spreading throughout Europe. It's an honorable campaign that will go down in history as the greatest war ever fought. And you gentlemen are part of it." Captain Fitzgerald took one more drag before emptying the pipe's burned-out contents into the ashtray.

"Somebody is going to have to pay for the damage to the pub, so it will be taken from your pay."

"Oh, come on, sir! That's not fair! Grasso blurted out. "There were a whole lot of other guys involved in that fight. Why should we be the ones to foot the bill?"

"Because you five were the only ones stupid enough to be caught by the MPs", Captain Fitzgerald snapped. "Now, is there anything else?"

We stood silent; I had a couple of questions to ask but did not want to push it.

"Now, I want you men to bury the hatchet and shake hands," Captain Fitzgerald said. The five of us hesitated. We just stared at each other, not wanting to be the first to offer hands. "Come on, men, I insist."

I was standing next to Ben and I definitely did not want to shake his hand. "Shake hands, now!" Captain Fitzgerald shouted. "That's an order. Or do you want to spend another night in the stockade?" The five of us vigorously shook hands. We had spent one night in jail and did not want to spend another. "All right, dismissed, except for Jenkins and Walton."

The three white soldiers quickly left the office, leaving Charles and me standing at attention. Captain Fitzgerald sat at the edge of his desk puffing on a pipe which had no tobacco in it.

"It's unfortunate what happened in that pub, but you two handled it badly. I'm not letting you off the hook. There's going to be problems such as this often. I'm not condoning it, but you have to handle it in a more reasonable way. If there's a problem out there that you think is unfair, you go to your superiors. You don't go charging in like a bull in a china shop. Is that understood?"

Charles and I said, "Yes, sir," in unison.

"You guys threw the first punch, so in addition to lost pay, I'm restricting both of you on base for two weeks. Dismissed."

We both saluted and went outside, feeling lucky that our punishment wasn't more severe. It was unfair that only Charles and I were restricted to base, but we both realized that was how black troops were treated. He said that we should have reported it, but if we had, nothing would have come from it. We knew that and he knew that. As we walked outside, we shielded our eyes from the bright sun. We put on our hats and were about to leave when Ben and his buddies approached us. They were waiting for us in front of a Jeep parked in front of headquarters. We both ignored them and started to walk past them. Ben placed his hand on my elbow, stopping me.

"Just because we shook hands in there, Sambo, don't make us friends," he said. I pushed his hand off my elbow.

"Yes, we did shake, and I'm going to make sure I wash my hands," I said.

"You're a real smart ass, aren't you?" He glanced over at Charles. "And you don't scare me with that Jap shit."

"Actually, it's Korean."

"I don't give a shit what it is. Why don't you fight like a real man? With your fists, instead of that judo or whatever that crap is."

Seymour stepped between us. "Come on, Ben, it's not worth it. Let's just forget about it and head back to the barracks." Ben nudged Seymour away and pointed a warning finger at us.

"You may be able to go where you want off post, but on post you better know your place."

With that, the three soldiers turned and walked away towards their barracks. Charles and I walked in the opposite direction. There was still a lot of military activity going on around the area. Truckloads of American soldiers and tanks were going up and down the dirt road.

"Hey, man, you were really great at that pub last night. Where did you learn to fight like that?" I asked.

Charles looked at me and smiled. "Back home I did some training in a local gym, some boxing and tae kwon do."

"You think you can teach me some of those moves?" I asked.

Charles smiled once again. "It's not something you learn overnight. It takes a lot of training and patience."

"Patience is one thing I have. Come on, it doesn't have to be anything intense. Just show me a few basic moves."

"Tell you what. I train at the gym on post every day. I'll show you some tricks, all right?"

"Hey, I'll be there. What time?"

"Five."

"I'll be there."

We shook hands and parted ways. Charles went to his unit, and I went to mine.

CHAPTER 19

It was a makeshift gym that consisted of a wall pulley, a ping-pong table, and a small baseball field out back. There was a mat in the middle of the floor. Soldiers went there for work outs, rest, or recreation. I'd been meeting Charles there for three days. I worked out on the mat for an hour, sometimes an hour and a half. Charles showed me some basic moves, like flipping an opponent, or disarming him. We mainly did kicking and punching exercises. I wanted to learn his moves, but he told me it took a lot of training and practice to get to the level he was at, which was a black belt. We both were restricted to base, so we had a lot of time on our hands. While most of the other soldiers went off base on their off-duty hours, we stayed playing cards or checkers. We even saw an occasional movie. One day Charles, Bubba, and I were having lunch in the mess hall.

"That was some fight we had the other night," Bubba said.

"Winston talked us right into a fight but when it started he was nowhere to be found," I said with a mouthful of baked beans.

"You handled yourself pretty good out there, Charles. What was that, karate?" Bubba asked.

"No, it's called *tae kwon do*."

"So how long are you guys stuck on base?"

"About another week," I replied. "How did you guys get out of that pub so fast?"

"Lucky, I guess. The first sign of those MPs, me and Winston jumped out the side window."

We finished our lunch and took our trays and placed them on the counter for the KP detail to take care of. On our way out, Bubba noticed three Women's Army Corps members, (WACs) sitting at a table.

"Wait a minute, fellas." He sauntered up to the table and looked closely at the woman in the middle.

"Annabelle?" he asked.

The woman looked at Bubba, then smiled broadly. "Bubba, is that you?" She leapt from the table and gave Bubba a huge hug.

"My, oh my, this is a small world!" she exclaimed. "I heard you joined the army, but I didn't think I'd bump into you out here."

"I thought you were stateside, in South Carolina," Bubba said. "How long have you been here?"

"We just got here. I want you to meet my two friends, Janet, and Lorraine."

"Nice meeting you two ladies. And I want you to meet Charles and Walter. Walter, Charles, this is my cousin Annabelle."

We all sat at the table and chatted for a while. Bubba made a date to take his cousin and her friends out to show them the sites. Charles and I were invited, but we couldn't go because we were restricted to the base.

***

One of the disadvantages of being restricted to base was that you had to pull extra duties. I had to pick up the mail from headquarters and bring it to the army post office on base. The next day, I brought in two bags of mail. A private took the bags from me and began sorting the mail into different slots in the wall. I was about to leave when I heard someone calling my name. I turned and saw a female soldier. She had a familiar face, but I couldn't place it.

"You don't remember me, do you?" she asked.

I looked closer at her, then shrugged my shoulders. "You do look familiar," I said.

"I'm Annabelle's friend. We met at the mess hall yesterday."

"Oh, yeah. Lorraine, right?"

"That's me," she said, smiling.

"I thought Bubba was showing you and Annabelle around town?"

"He's showing Janet and Annabelle around. I got stuck here, doing inventory."

"Inventory?"

"Yeah, there's going to be a big inspection tomorrow, and I want to be ready." I found myself looking at how she looked in her class-A dress uniform and couldn't help wondering how she would look in a regular dress or a bathing suit.

"That's a shame you didn't get a chance to see the town," I said. "I would show you around town if I could, but I'm restricted to base."

"Well, to tell you the truth, since I'm new here, I haven't seen much of the base."

Now that was a hint I couldn't pass up. "How about I show you around base after you get off?" I asked.

She accepted, and a couple of hours later we went to the enlisted men's club. It was opened to Negroes that night, so we stopped in for a drink. I told her I was from Harlem, New York. Turned out she was from New York also. She was born in Brooklyn, but her family moved to Chicago when her father found a better job. I was still thinking of Gwen, and I didn't want to get serious with anyone at this time. But I enjoyed talking to Lorraine. We were just two friends talking and having a drink. She told me she was stationed in Birmingham, England about 160 miles from where we were. She was with the 6888th Postal Division, an all-black female unit headed by Major Charity Early, the highest-ranking black female officer in the army. Lorraine and the other two female soldiers had been sent to this base temporarily to oversee the mail system. They would be here only a couple of weeks, and then it was back to the main branch in Birmingham.

I would see her around the post or in the mess hall and we would talk. We had some things in common: both our parents were from Jamaica, and we both liked history. Slowly, I found myself becoming attracted to her, I promised myself that I wouldn't get involved with another woman for a while, but there I was, liking the way she laughed and expressed herself. I found myself volunteering to bring mail to the post office just to see her. A few days after we talked, I stopped by and she was showing a group of soldiers the correct way to slot the mail. I had three bags of mail that I placed on the table.

"Hello, Walter. Is that it for the day?" she asked.

"That's it," I replied.

"Today is your last day being restricted to base, isn't it?"

"Yes, this is my last day. I can't wait to get off post."

"This is my last week on post, you know. Me and the girls are heading back Birmingham in six days."

I felt my heart sink. No, not now, I thought. I would hate to see her go just when I was starting to have feelings for her. I wasn't sure how she felt about me.

"I have a week left, so what are you going to do about it?" she asked coyly. What! I thought. I was confused about what she was trying to say.

"I see the way you look at me, Walter. When are you going to ask me out?"

***

There was a lot of activity on base. The soldiers who came in after us were sent to France to continue the fight. It looked like the war would be over soon, and we wouldn't be seeing any action. To me, it was a godsend; to the rest of the men, it was a disappointment.

I was going to take Lorraine out on a real date and I wanted it to be special. I had just about forgotten all about Gwen; she was a distant memory. I was on my way to pick up Lorraine when I remembered I had *tae kwon do* training with Charles. I stopped at the gym to let him know I couldn't make it.

"You can't make it? Charles complained. "I wish you had let me know sooner."

"Sorry, Charles, but I got this hot date with Lorraine."

"I thought you two were just friends."

"It blossomed into something else."

"You said you were giving up on women."

"I'm not going to give up forever."

Charles seemed upset that I called off my training, but I went on my date with Lorraine undaunted. We met off post at a quaint little restaurant in town. My pay was small, due to the money they took out to pay for damages to the pub, but I had money saved for Gwen's engagement ring, so I figured I might as well use some of it. The meal was superb. It had been a while since Lorraine and I had restaurant food. It was a big difference compared to what we got in the mess hall. We had a nice bottle of wine with our pasta and shrimp. We were finishing up our meal when I heard sirens in the background.

"What's that?" I asked.

"That's the alarm alerting us that German bombers are in the area. We need to take cover!"

I was surprised that German bombers were here at this stage of the war. At the beginning the Germans had bombed

England, particularly London, constantly. Now the war had been brought close to the German border, so they were no longer on offense, they were on defense. They were desperately defending themselves and rarely came to London.

"Come on!" she shouted, "There's a shelter outside."

Some of the patrons in the restaurant went down to the basement. Lorraine and I went to a bomb shelter with many other civilians. The bombers continued to another town, and the all-clear was given. We left the bomb shelter hand-in-hand, laughing and talking.

CHAPTER 20

We were on our way to a pub, when a military Jeep with a staff sergeant pulled up beside us. "Sergeant Carter?" he asked.

"Yes," Lorraine said.

"I was told to come get you. We need you at the post office right away."

"I'm off duty, sergeant. Can't you get one of the other girls?"

"We can't locate them, and the captain told me to see if I could find you."

"Is it important?"

"We're having trouble with the file locator. I'm sorry to bother you, ma'am, but it's essential that you come. The captain said he'll make it up to you."

Lorraine turned to me, disappointed that our first date was cut short. "Can I take a rain check Walter?"

"Sure. We can make it up another time."

"Do you want a ride back to base?" she asked.

"No, thanks. I've been stuck on base for two weeks. I'm going to hang around town for a little while longer." She gave me a quick peck on the lips, and she and the sergeant drove off.

I went over to the pub where my buddies and I had that fight and saw the bartender setting up bottles and glasses. He looked up and saw me walking in. "What are you doing here?" he asked.

"The door was open," I replied.

"I don't want you or your friends in here after what happened the other night."

"Calm down, will you? We paid for all the damages, didn't we?"

"You guys didn't even cover half the cost. But I'm willing to eat the loss. But from now on, I don't want whites and blacks mixing in here. I can't afford it. So, on certain nights it will be blacks only, and other nights, whites only."

I nodded my head and walked out without saying a word. How could I blame him? He was a businessman trying to make a living. It was a shame. Before we arrived, anyone could come into the pub. But now, we Americans came in with our race issues, giving this man no other choice but to segregate his customers. I saw the night club across the street that Charles and his friend went to a couple of weeks ago, Ole Brothers Place. I crossed the street to check it out. When I walked in, I was surprised by the number of men circulating around the place. There were no women that I could see. Maybe it was a gentlemen's club. I looked around and spotted Charles sitting at a table with the same guy I had seen him with two weeks ago. I walked over to the table and sat down. They were both startled when they saw me.

"What's up, Charles?" I asked.

"What are you doing here? Did you follow me?"

"I was surprised at the question but disregarded it. "No, I remembered seeing you leave this place a couple of weeks ago and thought I'd check it out."

At that point, an odd little man sat next to me at the table. He had his hair combed back and packed with grease. He had some type of rouge on his cheeks and an overpowering fragrance of cologne. He was smoking a cigarette with a holder on the filter. He looked me up and down. "Who's your friend, Charles?" he asked. Charles seemed uneasy.

"Go away, Stanley, he's not interested."

Stanley took a long drag on his cigarette and stared at me.

"Well, I saw the three of you sitting here and thought I'd come over and even things out. What's that saying in America? 'Two is company, and three's a crowd?'"

"Just go, will you? Charles snorted.

The strange man stood and stared at me intensely. He took another drag on his cigarette, then pointed at the bar. "If you need company, I'll be over there at the bar," he said. He walked over to the bar and started conversing with other patrons. I wanted to get away from this awkward situation.

"I'm going to the rest room." I said. I got up and started for the bathroom. As I walked in, I noticed two men against the wall. I paid no attention to them and went straight to the urinal. After I finished, I noticed the two men kissing and rubbing against each other. It then occurred to me that this place was a club for homosexuals. I had heard about places like this. We had a few of them in New York, but I'd never been inside one before. I briskly made my way back to the table to alert Charles.

"Charles!" I said desperately. We've got to go!"

"Calm down, Walter." I put my hand on his elbow to escort him out. Charles looked at the man sitting across from him. "I'll be back, Justin," he said. Justin smiled weakly and continued drinking his wine. Charles and I went outside. I was rushing him through the door.

"Do you know what this place is?" I asked. Before Charles could answer, I continued. "It's a homosexual club, a bathhouse. We've got to get out of here."

"I'm staying, Walter."

"Did you hear what I said? This is a fag joint."

"*I AM A FAG*! Charles shouted.

I was completely stunned by his outburst. My army buddy was a homosexual. I couldn't believe it. All that time we had spent together on post, playing chess, checkers, going to the movies, and training at the gym, and I never knew. I was in a daze. I just stood there, looking at him in disbelief.

"How long have you been like this?" I asked, still shocked.

Charles couldn't keep himself from laughing. "Just about all my life."

"But you don't look or act like one."

"Believe me, Walter, I am."

"Can't you get some sort of help? Maybe a psychiatrist? I heard they can do wonders."

"There' nothing a psychiatrist can do for me. This is who I am."

I stood there in semi-shock, but the numbness was beginning to fade away. "So why didn't you tell me?"

"Do you know what would happen to me if it ever got out that I'm gay? You have to be straight in the army; otherwise, it's an immediate discharge. And I don't want that." He placed his hand on my shoulder. "We can still be friends." I looked at his hand on my shoulder, glanced at him, and then looked at my shoulder again. He withdrew his hand and waited for a response from me. I had none. "Look, Walter. Promise me you won't tell anybody, all right?"

I nodded my head and walked away, disappointed. I looked back to see what Charles was going to do and saw him walk back into the club. I turned away but stopped and looked at him one last time. It was like I had lost my best friend. I continued toward the base in a daze.

CHAPTER 21

When I returned to base, I went to my bunk and slumped on my bed. Most of the men were still off base. The only one present was Tank. He was lying on his bunk, reading an old issue of Stars and Stripes. He looked at me while I lay down on my bed.

"What's the matter with you?" he asked.

"What makes you think there's something wrong?"

"Come on, Walter. I've known you for over six months now. I know when something's bothering you."

I sat up on my bed and looked at Tank. This thing was eating at me and I needed to get it off my chest. I needed to tell somebody, and it might as well be him. "Listen, Tank. I'm gonna tell you something and you have to promise not to breathe a word of this to anyone."

Tank dropped his newspaper and sat on the bunk next to me, eager to hear some gossip. "You have my word, man. Go ahead, tell me."

I told him about Ole Brothers Place and the clientele who hung out there, and that Charles was a homosexual and had a boyfriend named Justin. He sat there as shocked as I was when I first found out.

"No, shit," he said. "Are you sure?"

"Positive. And the only reason I'm telling you this is because you're from Boston."

"What does Boston have to do with it?"

"Well, I heard Boston is a liberal town that's open-minded about matters like this."

"I don't know where you get all your information from. Boston is no different from New York or any other Northern state. I'm just as baffled as you are. And he fights so well, I just don't believe it." "You have to promise me, Tank, not to tell anybody."

"My lips are sealed."

The next morning, I was in the chow line in the mess hall getting breakfast. I sat at the table with

Bay Bay, Winston, and the rest of the group. Everyone was there except Charles. Bubba and Winston were horsing around as usual, and Tank and Bay Bay were engaged in general conversation. I just sat there, quietly thinking about what happened last night between me and Charles.

"What's wrong?" Winston asked.

"Nothing," I replied.

"You haven't said ten word since you got here. What's the matter, you thinking about that postal chick you've been dating?"

"I just have things on my mind, that's all. I'll catch you guys later."

I got up from the table and was about to leave, when I saw Charles coming toward me with a tray of food. I walked in the opposite direction to avoid him. The rest of the day consisted of maintaining our equipment and firearms. Another white battalion was shipped out, a group that arrived after we did. It looked more and more like we were not going to see any action, which did not bother me one bit. The rest of the week was the same routine of keeping our gear and equipment in tip top shape. One morning I was taking a shower in the stall next to Bubba and Bay Bay. They finished and dried themselves and went to the bunk area. I continued washing myself, when Charles came in and used the shower next to me.

"Hello, Walter," he said. "I haven't seen you in a while."

I was shocked to see Charles standing next to me, naked. I immediately covered myself with a towel. "What are you doing here? You don't belong here, you're with the 458th."

"Their showers are on the blink. We were told to come here." I made sure I was covered before I started to make my way out. "What's the matter, Walter? I didn't know you were so shy."

"I'm not. I just don't like men checking me out."

"Don't flatter yourself; I'm not checking you out. You missed your training yesterday. You haven't been at the gym all week."

"I'm not going anymore. I'm giving it up," I said.

"Does it have anything to do with me being gay?"

"Why didn't you come clean with me when we first met and told me you were this way?"

"It's something I shouldn't be talking about."

"I can understand you not wanting to talk about it, but you didn't have to mislead me."

"How do you figure that I misled you?"

"When we first met, you told me that you had broken up with your girlfriend."

"You assumed it was my girlfriend. It actually was my boyfriend."

I shook my head in dismay. "This is all too weird for me."

"Look, Walter, there's no reason why we still can't be friends."

"Are you kidding? If word gets out that you're gay, people are gonna assume that I am too."

"Who cares what people think."

"I care, I have a reputation. Why did you want to be my friend anyway?"

"It was something that just happened," Charles said.

"Of all the guys in the battalion, you wanted to hang out with me."

Charles finished showering and began drying himself. "I'll admit I was attracted to you at first, but I realized that nothing could ever happen between us. I met this nice man in town named Justin, and I'm completely in love with him. So, there's no reason why we can't be friends."

"You see, that's what I'm talking about. You have no business being attracted to me in the first place."

"That's the problem with you heterosexuals - you're so uptight. Why don't you just take it as a compliment?"

I shook my head, confused about the situation. "This is so weird."

Tank came into the shower stall. He was about to disrobe but saw Charles and me standing there. "Am I interrupting anything?" he asked.

I was ashamed that Tank saw us together. He was the only one I told that Charles was a homosexual. I walked out of the stall without saying a word.

CHAPTER 22

It was another day at the mess hall. I was having breakfast with Lorraine. It was the first time we had seen each other since our last date got cut short. The meal consisted of fried eggs, grits, and bacon.

"I'm going back to Birmingham in a few days," she said.

"How about we have dinner at that nice restaurant in town?" I asked. While I was waiting for an answer, Charles came into the mess hall. He got a tray of food and was proceeding to a table, when he spotted me. He waved, but I ignored him.

"That was rude," Lorraine said.

"I don't want anything to do with that guy," I replied.

"Why?"

I looked around to make sure no one was listening. I moved my head closer to hers and lowered my voice. "He's a homosexual."

"He is? How did you know?"

"He told me."

"That's interesting."

She continued drinking her coffee. I looked at her, amazed. "Interesting? Is that all you have to say?"

"Is there more that I should say? He should keep this lifestyle of his quiet if he doesn't want to get kicked out of the army."

"What about me? If word gets out that he's a homo, people are going to think that I'm one too."

"Who cares what people think, Walter."

"If the brass thinks that I'm that way, I could get kicked out."

"No, you wouldn't. You can't get kicked out just like that. They'd have to have proof."

"In any case, I'm staying away from him."

"How can you be like that, so closed-minded? He's supposed to be your friend."

"Friends like that I don't need."

"Friends don't just grow on trees, Walter."

"It's easy for you to say, you don't have to put up with it."

"I've put up with it just about all my life. I had an aunt who was like that, and I still love her.
She's my aunt and will always be my aunt, regardless."

"If it ever gets out that he's a homo, everyone will think that I'm one too. I just can't deal with that."

"What about your white friend, Red?"

"What does he have to do with this?"

"You told me all about him, how he stuck up for you when that white soldier called him a nigger lover. He was ready to fight for you. He didn't worry about what other white soldiers thought of him. All he knew was that you were his friend and he was willing to stand up for that principle." "That's different." said walter.

"How is it different?"

"There's a big difference between being black and being a homosexual."

"That's not the point, Walter. I'm talking about being a friend, but that's something you seem to know nothing about. Maybe you should take some lessons from Red." She drank the rest of her coffee and placed the cup on her tray. "I have to go now. I'll see you."

She got up from the table with her tray and walked away without any further comment. I remained seated, pondering what she said. No matter how I looked at it, I realized she had a valid point.

That afternoon I went to the gym and found Charles going through his martial arts routine. I walked up to him and tapped him on the shoulder. He turned, then ignored me and continued with his workout, going through his kicking and punching movements.

"What's happening, Charles?" I asked. He ignored me and continued with his exercise routine.
"So, you're going to snub me now after all we've been through?"

He stopped exercising, picked up a towel, and wiped the sweat from his forehead. He was wearing gray sweatpants and a white T-shirt. "Aren't you afraid of being seen talking with the local fairy?" He proceeded to go through his martial arts motions, doing front high kicks and forward punches. "What do you want, Walter?"

"It's five o'clock, time for my training."

"I thought you quit."

"I changed my mind."

"You can't keep changing your mind. Once you get started, you have to stick with it."

"I plan to," I replied.

I took off my army boots and shirt and proceeded to exercise alongside him.

CHAPTER 23

Being friends with Charles was not the same as it had been before. I still felt a bit awkward around him and his friends. Whenever he glanced at me or casually touched my arm, I wondered if he was flirting with me. Lorraine on the other hand, was completely at ease with Charles and Justin. I took her to Ole Brothers Place, where she seemed to fit right in. Seeing men dancing with men didn't seem to faze her. I guess she was used to it seeing that her aunt was a lesbian. When Lorraine and I danced, we were the only straight couple in the place. But that didn't seem to bother anyone. I got to know Charles's boyfriend, Justin, a little better and found him to be a decent guy. He had bought an old coffee shop before the war from a family inheritance and turned it into a gay bar and named it My Brothers Place. He changed the name a few years later to Ole Brothers Place. He had joined the British Army during the blitz in London and was stationed over in Africa. He had left the club for Stanley to watch over while he served in the military. He was wounded and then discharged, and had lived in Wimborne ever since. He told me that ever since he was a child, he knew that he was different from other little boys. He wanted to play with dolls and jump rope with the girls while boys his age were playing soldier or rugby.

I walked Lorraine to the female quarters on the post. We were holding hands when we arrived, it was late at night. An army Jeep and a truck full of soldiers passed by.

"I'll be leaving the day after tomorrow," she said.

"Listen, Lorraine. Charles and Justin were telling me about this nice little inn not too far from here. You think it might be possible for us to spend some time at that inn tomorrow?"

"All right." she said.

We kissed goodnight, and she went inside. For the rest of that night and the following day, I was floating on air. I was going to get a weekend pass, and Lorraine and I had big plans. Justin made reservations at the inn for Lorraine and me. Charles and Justin were going to get their own room not far from ours. After spending the rest of the day going through our grueling training, I was having dinner in the mess hall with Charles. We had the rest of the night planned out. The two rooms were already reserved. I was to meet Charles off post, where we would hail a cab. We would ride down to Ole Brothers Place to pick up Lorraine and Justin. I had heard Lorraine had a special dress picked out. We would then drive to the inn to spend a glorious weekend together, then drive back to post in time for her to catch her ride to Birmingham. At three o'clock, I finally received my weekend pass. I rushed to the barracks for a quick shower and shave. I splashed on some after shave and a touch of cologne behind my ears. My dress uniform was pressed and starched. Winston was in the bathroom and had just finished using the toilet.

"Hot date tonight, huh, Walter?" Winston asked.

"Yeah, you can say that."

I walked into the bunk area combing my hair. Bubba was on the top bunk shining his boots. Bay Bay was sitting on the bottom bunk brushing his hair, and Tank was lying on his bunk reading a magazine. As I was making my way to the door, I heard some snickering in the background. I ignored it and continued on my way, when Bubba let out a loud cat whistle.

"Shake it, baby! he shouted.

I stopped and turned. I strolled up to him. "You got something to say?"

"No, I got nothing to say," he said, snickering.

Tank stopped reading his magazine and stood upright. Bay Bay put his brush down and was attentive to what was developing.

"I'm just saying you sure are looking fine." There was more laughter. Winston came up behind me. "Who are you going out with? Your girlfriend Lorraine or your boyfriend Charles?"

I was beginning to get hot around the collar, but I maintained my cool. I looked at Tank, but he averted eye contact. He was the only one I had told that Charles was a homosexual, and now he had told my bunkmates.

"Why don't you guys knock it off. Charles is just a friend, that's all."

Bubba jumped down from his top bunk. "There's talk going around that he's a fag."

"Hey! We're just friends, all right?"

"Yeah, I bet you are," Bubba snickered. "I heard you two were getting awfully cozy in the shower yesterday."

"I don't know where you're getting all your information from. We just happened to bump into each other. The showers over at his barracks were broken, so he had to use ours."

"What about those special evenings at the gym?"

"All he's doing is showing me some karate moves."

Bubba let go another loud laugh. "What kind of moves is he teaching you? Are you the pitcher or the catcher?"

"You got something to say, Bubba? Why don't you just spit it out?"

"I got nothing to say, Walter. If this is the lifestyle you choose, so be it. Let it not be said that I stood between a man and his man." Thunderous laughter broke out in the room. Bubba took his fingers and pinched my cheeks. "You have a good time now, lover boy." This was about as much as I could stand. I took his hand and flung it from my face.

"You keep your damn hands to yourself."

Bay Bay provoked the situation. "Whoa, Bubba. You gonna take that?"

Bubba was still laughing. "I'm going to have to. He might scratch my eyes out or hit me with his purse."

Everybody in the room was laughing. I turned and was about to storm out, when Bubba slapped me on my buttocks. Without thinking, I reacted by giving him a right jab square on his face. He staggered back, blood spurting from his nose. He held his nose to contain the bleeding. He looked at me, his face contorted with rage as he began taking off his fatigue shirt. "It's going to be that way, huh? Let's get it on then."

He balled his hands into a fist and went into a boxing stance, moving side to side and back and forth. He swung widely at me, missing my face by inches. I managed to avoid being hit by moving my head to the side. I tried a karate move that Charles had taught me, planting my left foot firmly on the ground and coming around with my right foot. I guess I wasn't quite good at it; Bubba caught my foot in mid-air and flung me against the locker. He got his arms around me and buried his cheek into my shoulders, making it difficult for me to hit him. He wrestled me to the ground, placing his knee on my stomach, trying to hold me down. I somehow managed to twist to the side and spring back to my feet. I hit him with a left hook and a right cross, and he went backwards. He came forward with an overhand right punch that I blocked with my left hand, but he came back with a devastating left hook that caught me off guard. It was a powerful punch. My legs felt like jelly, they wobbled, and I fell on my backside.

"Get up!" he shouted.

I remained on the floor trying to regain my composure. He reached down and grabbed me by my collar and heaved me to my feet. I was still dazed but I wasn't about to give up. I gave him an uppercut under his chin. This enraged him, and he came back with a left hook, then a right. Blood spurted from my nose and mouth. He continued with his barrage of punches, to my face, midsection, and ribs. I blacked out. When I regained consciousness, I was lying on a bed in the infirmary. My vision was blurred, but I managed to make out a nurse standing over me. I tried to get up, but my head was spinning and I lay back down.

"You're awake," she said. "I'll be right back."

She left and returned with a doctor. He put his hand over my forehead, then checked my eyes with a pen light.

"How do you feel? he asked. I attempted to get up, but the pain was too great, and my head was still spinning. I collapsed back on the bed. "Don't move," he said. You have a mild concussion plus some bruised ribs. You'll be here for a couple of days."

"What happened to the guy who put me here?" I asked.

"For now, he's in the stockade, but I wouldn't concern myself about that right now. Let's concentrate on you getting better." The doctor spoke to the nurse. She nodded her head. He then exited the room to attend to other patients.

"Is there anything I can get you?" she asked. I said no, and she left the room. I tried to move, but there was a lot of pain all over my body. Bubba really gave me a good beating, I thought. I attempted to roll over to my side, but the pain shot through my ribs, so I remained on my back. I thought of Lorraine and the day we had planned and realized she was probably halfway to Birmingham by now.

CHAPTER 24

Lorraine stopped by briefly to say good-bye. It was time for her to head back to Birmingham and she wanted to see me before she left. She was saddened to see me lying on the hospital bed, face all bruised up and battered. Although we didn't get a chance to spend the weekend together at the inn, we made plans to meet in Birmingham in a couple of weeks. She kissed me good-bye and rushed off to her waiting Jeep. None of the guys visited me. Tank, Winston, and Bay Bay avoided me like the plague. Rumors of Charles being gay spread around the base like wildfire, and my so-called friends were staying away from me; they didn't want to be associated with homosexuals. Charles later stopped by to see me. He stood over my bed shaking his head.

"If only I was there, I could have prevented this from happening," he said.

"Don't worry about it. What's done is done," I said.

"So, when are you getting out of here?"

"Tomorrow, then Bubba and I have to see Captain Fitzgerald."

"Is Bubba still in jail?"

"Yeah, the last I heard," I replied.

I appreciated Charles coming by to see me; no one else did. I was released the following day with orders from the doctor that I should be on light duty for a couple of weeks. I was dropped off at the barracks by a Jeep with a red cross on the hood. As I walked into the barracks, there was a lot of chattering going on. Everyone stopped talking when I walked in. I was still a little dizzy and made my way slowly to my bunk. I lay down without saying a word. Finally, Winston broke the silence and spoke up.

"So, how you feeling, Walter?"

Everyone else remained silent. I looked up at Winston. "Fine," I replied.

"I don't care if you are queer, you're still my buddy," he said.

"I'm not queer, you guys. Just because Charles is a homosexual, don't make me one. He's my friend, and that's it."

Bay Bay, whose bunk was next to mine, moved over to an empty bunk. "What's wrong with you?" I asked.

"Nothing. I just think its best that I sleep over here."

"You think I'm going to bother you while you're asleep?"

"I just don't want people razzing me, that's all," Bay Bay said.

"What gives with you guys? Are you deaf? Read my lips, I'm going to say it one more time. I'm not gay. You want me to have it notarized? They all just looked at me like I was an alien from outer space.

"We know for a fact that Charles is a fruitcake and you two been buddy-buddy the past couple of weeks," Tank said

"If I'm gay, what am I doing with Lorraine?"

"I heard of guys who can go both ways," Winston replied.

"Damn! I just can't win with you guys."

I was going to make my case further but decided against it. It wouldn't do any good. Those guys had it planted in their heads that I was a homosexual, and there was no way to make them think otherwise. My ribs were still sore, so I remained on my back. I closed my eyes to try to block these idiots out of my mind, when Bubba walked in. His face was a little roughed up by the blows I had managed to slip in, but it was nothing compared to what I looked like. He glanced over at me and went over to his footlocker. He opened it and started packing. The guys immediately surrounded him with greetings.

"How's it going?" Winston asked.

"When did you get out?" Tank asked.

"This afternoon," Bubba replied. "They're going to transfer me to another unit, all because of that sissy boy over there." He pointed at me. A flash of anger came over me, but I decided to remain silent. If Bubba and I got into another fight, it would probably kill me.

"That's a bum rap," Bay Bay said." He threw the first punch, and they punish you for it."

"That's a shame," Winston said. "We were one hell of a fighting team, now we're being separated."

I just sat there, feeling more depressed. Not only did my bunkmates think I was a homosexual, but they were blaming me for getting the most popular guy in our platoon transferred. I didn't think I could feel any lower, but I was wrong. Out of the corner of my eye, I saw Charles walk in. He strolled by the fellows and came straight to me. Everyone's attention was turned to us. There was silence as they looked on in bewilderment. Before I could say anything, Bubba spoke.

"Hey, guys, why don't we leave these two lovebirds alone." There was some laughter. Not as much as there was in our first encounter, but a small, nervous type laughter.

"Why don't you mind your own business, fathead," Charles snapped.

Bubba's laugh turned into a sudden frown.

"Let me tell you something, sissy boy," he said. "The only reason I don't go over there and bitchslap your ass is because I'm in enough trouble already."

Charles left my bedside and walked right up to Bubba. Winston, Tank, and Bay Bay made way for him as he went face-to-face with him. "The only reason you don't slap me is because you're afraid to."

"Afraid of you!" Bubba snorted. "Why don't you go away chump. I've had enough laughter for one day."

Suddenly, without provocation or warning, Charles slapped Bubba in the face. It startled everyone in the room, including me.

I looked in Bubba's eyes and saw not only surprise and shock, but something else - doubt. He remembered how Charles had handled himself in the pub against those white soldiers and he had qualms about retaliating. Charles struck him again with a back handed slap, and blood trickled down the corner of Bubba's lip. "Are you just going to stand there and bleed, or fight back?"

Bubba let out an animal-like yell and charged. Charles evaded him, moving to the side. Bubba swung a left, then a right. Charles ducked and dodged each punch like a master at his craft. Bubba charged again and was tripped up by Charles. He got back on his feet and threw a right. Charles caught his arm and flipped him over his back. I was in awe at the ease with which Charles was handling Bubba. Then it happened. Charles made his first mistake. He did a roundabout kick to Bubba's face, just missing him. His left side was exposed, and Bubba took advantage of the opening. He hit Charles with a hard right to his left side. Charles doubled over. Bubba then let go with a left cross to his face. Everyone in the room leapt for joy as Charles backed away, in obvious trouble.

"Get him, Bubba!" Bay Bay yelled.

"You got him, Bubba!" Winston shouted.

"Nail him, Bubba," Tank said.

I could see that Charles was dazed. He grabbed on to Bubba so he couldn't get another punch in, something boxers do sometimes to gain some time to get their composure back. Bubba pushed him away and came back with a devastating right that just missed Charles's head. If it had connected, I would have been picking Charles's head up from the ground. Bubba came back with a left jab, again missing Charles, hitting the locker instead and leaving a huge dent. Life seemed to gradually creep back into Charles. He slowly regained his composure. The spring in his legs was coming back. He danced around some more before coming in with a straightforward karate punch that Bubba tried to block, but it caught him on the nose. Charles backed up, then came forward and leaped in the air, hitting Bubba in the face. Bubba backed up, dazed. Charles landed on the floor, and in a circular motion, swept his leg under Bubba, causing him to fall.

The guys in the room fell silent as Bubba gingerly made it back to his feet. Charles immediately planted his left foot squarely on the floor, then came around with his right foot, hitting Bubba on the side of his face. Bubba's eyes were glassy as he weakly tried to swing a right cross. Charles countered with punches to Bubba's mid-section and face. Bubba seemed disoriented as Charles planted his foot on the floor and thrust a left side kick squarely to Bubba's chest; he soared backwards, his back slamming against a locker. Bubba slumped to the floor, raising his hand to signal that he had had enough. Charles then turned to the men in the barracks. He was still favoring his left side, holding it as he walked by. He stopped and turned around. "Anybody else got something to say?"

No one said anything. Charles continued out the door and outside. Winston and Tank helped Bubba to his feet. Humiliated, Bubba said nothing and sat on his bunk. I didn't know whether to be happy or sad. I was glad to see Bubba taken down a notch, but it was going to look like Charles came back to protect his boyfriend's honor. The guys in the room looked at me but said nothing. They all thought I was gay, but I just didn't care anymore.

CHAPTER 25

We were at battalion headquarters, scheduled to see Captain Fitzgerald. The clerk had Charles and me sit on the wooden bench outside his office. The clerk continued with his duties, typing reports on his desk. The captain already had Bubba in his office, probably chewing him out. He opened the door, pointed to Charles, and motioned with his finger for him to come in. Charles stood up and made his way into the office.

"You, too," Captain Fitzgerald said, pointing his finger at me. "I want both of you in my office."

I got up and followed Charles. Bubba was still standing at attention in front of the desk. Captain Fitzgerald did not dismiss Bubba. He wanted all three of us in his office. I was a little surprised. I thought he was going to see us one at a time. We stood at attention next to Bubba, looking straight ahead. Captain Fitzgerald closed the door and walked in front of us, looking at each of us while shaking his head. He looked directly at me and Charles.

"The last time you two were here, I had to reprimand you for that bar fight. Now you're here again for fighting. You fought white soldiers, now you're fighting your own kind. Is there anyone that you two bozos can get along with?" We stood at attention, not wanting to answer a rhetorical question. He took out his pipe and began packing it with tobacco.

"Now listen up gentlemen, because I'm only going to say this one time. If I see you in this office again for fighting, you will be court-martialed. I will not tolerate this kind of behavior. Why don't you save all that fighting energy for the Jerries? Now, this is going to be your last warning. Three strikes and you're out. Am I making myself clear?"

All three of us replied, "Yes, sir," in unison.

He stood there a moment and eyed each of us, especially Charles. "Jenkins and Walton, stay put.

Bubba, you're dismissed."

Bubba quickly saluted the captain and did an about face. He glanced at me and Charles before exiting the office. Captain Fitzgerald lit his pipe, something he always did before he went into a lecture. "Stand at ease, men." We both placed our hands behind our backs and spread our legs apart. "I'm not one to go around listening to rumors," he said, "but what I'm hearing is very disturbing." He took a drag on his pipe and blew smoke from his nose. "Now, I'm not going to beat around the bush, I'm going to come right out and ask. Are you two a couple of fags?"

Charles and I were taken aback by the abruptness of his question. "I believe the correct terminology is 'homosexual' sir," Charles said.

"You're out of line, soldier, "Captain Fitzgerald admonished. Don't correct me when I'm speaking. Now, answer the question."

Charles and I answered, "No, sir," in unison.

"Because if you are, that is immediate discharge. You're aware of that, aren't you?"

Again, in unison, we both said, "Yes, sir."

"We are about to go into battle, gentlemen, and I don't want to have to handle this out on the battlefield. So, I'll make a deal with you. If you admit to your homosexuality, I'll guarantee an honorable discharge. But if I find out that you two are queer when we're out on the battlefield, I will do everything in my power to make sure you receive a dishonorable discharge. Am I making myself clear, gentlemen?"

"Again, we said, "Yes, sir."

"So, what's it going to be?" he asked.

This was tempting. If I said I was a homosexual, I could get out right away; I could be home with an honorable discharge in my pocket. I would be back in New York City, working at my old job, and I wouldn't be risking my life for this white man's war. But on the other hand, could I trust him? How did I know there wouldn't be something in my record stating that I was gay? I'd be marked as a homosexual for the rest of my life. It was a chance I wouldn't take.

"I'm not a homo, sir," I said.

He then turned his attention to Charles, waiting for his answer.

"Neither am I, sir," Charles said.

Captain Fitzgerald seemed disappointed. He eyed the both of us, trying to figure us out. He took another drag on his pipe. "All right, have it your way. I'm going to transfer Bubba to the 458th. "Walton, I want you over at the 761st, but I don't want you two sharing the same tank. So I want the two of you in separate platoons. Jenkins remains in Charlie Company, Walton will be in Bravo. And from now on that homo club Ole Brothers Place is off limits to all GIs is that understood?"

We both said, "Yes, sir."

"Dismissed."

We both saluted the Captain. He returned the salute, and we exited his office. As we passed the clerk, who was sitting at his desk shuffling paperwork, I could have sworn he was smiling. We went outside and noticed there was more activity than usual.

"Why didn't you take his offer?" Charles asked.

"Why should I? I'm not gay."

"It doesn't matter, it would have gotten you out. I know how much you hate being here. You could've been free and clear."

"To tell you the truth, I was thinking about it, but I don't trust the captain. There might have been something on my discharge papers labeling me as a homosexual. Why didn't you take the offer? You *are* gay."

"I don't know. I guess I like what I'm doing, being part of something."

Charles went to his old unit to start packing his gear. I went to my barracks and saw Bubba leaving with his duffel bag. We said nothing as we passed each other.

CHAPTER 26

At morning formation, we got the news that we had gotten our orders to ship out. We were going to France and into battle. They put us under lockdown. All weekend passes and leaves were cancelled. I tried to get in touch with Lorraine via telephone, but I couldn't get through. I had to see her one more time before shipping out. Things were tight on base. We were loading equipment and supplies on trucks, when I got the idea of sneaking off post to see her. But that would be impossible; there were a number of military police making their rounds and making sure GIs were in their proper units. As much as I wanted to, I didn't get to see her before we shipped out.

It was early morning when we began to cross the English Channel toward France. A group of landing ship tanks slowly cruised over the water at ten miles per hour. The LSTs were 328 feet long and 50 feet wide. Each ship could carry about twenty Sherman tanks on the deck or below the hull. Most of the 761ST crowded on the decks of the LSTs to catch a glimpse of the coast of France. We landed on Omaha Beach, a code name given to it during the D-Day invasion. This five-mile section of beach had the heaviest causalities; three thousand men had been killed or seriously injured in a short period of time. As we rode our tanks off the ramp of the boat, I marveled at the skeletal remains of tanks, trucks, and equipment left on the beach after the initial invasion. The human causalities had been removed, but the damaged equipment remained, a reminder of the fierce battle that had taken place four months earlier.

The MPs guarded us at a section of the beach where all tanks were gathered in formation, awaiting further orders. There were seventy-four medium and light tanks and over seven hundred African American soldiers checking and rechecking their weapons and equipment. We were later informed that we would be going to Les Pieux, a small town that was the battle front of the campaign. We were to link up with Patton's Twenty-Sixth Infantry, an all-white unit that was meeting heavy resistance from the Germans.

We packed our gear and began our four-hundred-mile journey east. We passed through cities and towns that had already been liberated by the allies. French men and women stood at their windows, cheering us on. Crowds of people cheered as we passed through, throwing flowers and waving French and American flags. Although I had never fired a shot, I felt somewhat like a hero. I stood in the tank turret, waving back at the jubilant crowd and giving them the thumbs up.

We set up camp in a town not far from the front. Some of the men from the 761st went to visit a local brothel. I chose not to. There was something about paying for sex that was unappealing. It was more or less a business transaction instead of something romantic and intimate. Of course, the men in my platoon thought I didn't want to go because I was a homosexual. I gave up trying to convince them otherwise. The autographed picture of Billie Holiday that Toby had given to me was hanging on the tank wall next to a picture of Lena Horne, another popular black jazz singer. Bay Bay had managed to get that picture. The outside of our tank had the name Harlem Raiders stenciled on the side of the turret. Other tanks had names like the Widow Maker, Black Stallion, and Cool Stud. We continued east down the road toward the front lines. We could hear shells exploding in the distance like sporadic thunder. The farther east we traveled, the fewer civilians we encountered, a sign that we were getting closer to the front. We stopped at a small town I forget the name of and camped out.

We set up a defensive position with tanks covering our left and right flanks. Not that we needed to, but it was good practice for when we reached the front lines. I was sitting by a tank with Winston and Bay Bay, opening a can of C-rations. I was lucky, I had steak and potatoes. The steak tasted like Spam and the potatoes like mashed mush. A soldier from E Company was passing by with a couple of his buddies.

"Did you hear about Lieutenant Robinson?" he asked.

"No, what about him?" I asked.

"He was found not guilty."

"You're kidding. On all counts?" asked Winston.

"Yeah."

"Well doesn't that beat all?"

The soldiers continued walking down the path to their tank. Winston had just finished his c-rations of frank and beans.

"I don't believe it," he said. "On all counts."

"I guess it was worth standing up and fighting for your rights," Bay Bay said. "If I ever get out of this war alive and return to Fort Hood and one of those bus drivers tells me to sit in the back, I'm gonna do just what Lieutenant Robinson did, tell him where he can stuff it."

The next morning after breakfast, we were summoned to form a semi-circle. All 720 of us gathered around. Lieutenant Bates directed us to stand at attention. Jeeps armed with .50-caliber machine guns and filled with MPs made their entrance. A three-star general jumped out of one of the Jeeps. It was a gray day, and a light drizzle was coming down as the general was helped to the hood of one of the half-tracks by an MP. I noticed that the general had two pearl-handled pistols strapped to his belt, and it was then that I realized who he was. It was General George Patton, Old Blood and Guts himself. He looked shorter than he did in the news reels, but it was him. He looked around at the formation, then spoke.

"Men, you are the first Negro tankers ever to fight in the American army. I would never have asked for you if you weren't good. I have nothing but the best in my army. I don't care what color you are, so long as you go up there and kill those Kraut sons-of-bitches. Everyone has their eyes on you and is expecting great things from you. Most of all, your race is looking forward to your success. Don't let them down, and damn you, don't let me down! They say it is patriotic to die for your country. Well, let's see how many patriots we can make out of those German sons-of-bitches." He looked around, then concluded. "There is one thing you men will be able to say when you go home. You may all thank God that thirty years from now, when you are sitting with your grandson on your knees, and he asks, 'Grandfather, what did you do in World War II?' You won't have to say, I shoveled shit in Mississippi."

He stepped off the half-track and spoke to some of the men in the front formation. As I watched him speaking, I had a feeling of satisfaction. Maybe I was doing something worthwhile, judging by the crowd cheering us on as liberators, and a world famous general taking the time to speak to us. Maybe the men in my battalion were right, maybe this wasn't just a white man's war after all, but a war for every race and nationality to fight. For the first time since joining the army, I felt a sense of honor and pride.

CHAPTER 27

The exploding shells were deafening as we gradually worked our way up the German lines. The resistance was fierce as the Germans threw everything they had at us. Winston had his eyes pressed to the periscope, guiding me through the muddy terrain. I looked through my periscope and could see traces of bullets whizzing at us and bouncing harmlessly off the tank. Although the bullets were doing no harm, they were fired on us for tracer fire so the heavier 75mm or 88s could zero in on us. They were deadly anti-tank weapons used by the Germans.

Winston adjusted his glasses and peeked through the periscope again to find a worthwhile target to take out. The order was given for us to fire smoke bombs to help conceal our position. Bay Bay immediately loaded a canister into the chamber and fired. The bomb exploded about three hundred meters in front of us, making it difficult for the Germans to see us, but it also made it difficult for me to see them or our target. Some men from the Twenty-Sixth Infantry were ahead of us. Some were mowed down by enemy gunfire, but they continued. I admired their courage. I looked through my periscope again and could see nothing through the smoke and mayhem.

"All right, I see something up ahead. Load up!" Winston shouted.

Bay Bay quickly yanked a heavy explosive shell from the turret wall and rammed it into the breech. The heavy gun fired, ejecting the spent shell. Bay Bay immediately reloaded, and the gunner fired again. The tank recoiled but continued eastward against earsplitting crashes of incoming shells. I noticed a slope in the ground and slowed the tank down.

"What's the matter?" Winston asked.

"I don't like that slope up ahead. There could be a tank trap down there." I replied.

An infantry soldier came up from the slope and gave the okay sign that it was clear to continue. I gunned the tank forward, and as we went down the slope there was an earsplitting explosion just above us. The tank shuddered and shook. A German anti-tank crew had zeroed in on us just as we went down the dip in the road. The missile missed the main body but sheared off the mount with the .50-caliber machine gun. The rest of the tank remained intact. If we hadn't gone down the dip when we had, it would have been a direct hit and all of us would have been killed. The near-death experience startled me, but I continued driving the tank. We came over the slope. The smoke was clearing and I could just barely make out the German lines from my periscope. As we got closer, I noticed a Panzer tank and an 88 anti-tank weapon on a hilltop just to the left of our position.

"Load up!" Winston shouted. "I'm gonna to try to take out that eighty-eight."

Just as Bay Bay threw another high explosive shell in the breech, there was a tremendous explosion next to us. A Panzer tank got a direct hit on a tank next to ours. One soldier managed to escape from the hatch, but the rest were trapped inside. You could hear their terrified screams as they were engulfed in the flaming inferno.

"Forget about the eighty-eight!" Winston shouted. "Let's get that Panzer."

The gunner swung the cannon around and shot a missile at the Panzer. The round bounced off the front hull. Bay Bay quickly reloaded another round in the chamber. Just as he was about to fire, there was an explosion underneath us that rocked the tank. The tank came to a sudden halt. I tried gunning the engine, but the tank went nowhere. We had run over a mine. The left track was blown off. I pressed my eye to the periscope and saw the Panzer tank adjusting its huge cannon and zeroing in on us. We could hear tracer fire pinging on the outside hull.

"We're sitting ducks!" Winston shouted. "Get the hell out of here!"

I made it over the hatch, followed by Winston, Bay Bay, and the gunner. Just as I made it over the top and landed on the ground, there was an enormous explosion, knocking me off my feet and throwing me about ten feet away. I was dazed and disoriented but knew I had to get away. Bullets exploded on the ground around me. I made a dash for a trench just ahead. I dove inside, my head hitting the bottom of the five-foot hole. I peeked over the top and saw puffs of smoke coming from cannons fired from the German lines. Being disoriented, I must have run in the wrong direction, because I was closer to the German lines than before. I looked behind me and saw no sign of the American lines or tanks or the advancing infantry. It was dusk and getting dark. If I wait here a little while longer, maybe I can make it back to the American lines under the cover of darkness, I thought.

I checked my sub machine gun and my .45 pistol. I had a full clip in my grease gun and eight bullets in my .45 pistol. I checked my body to see if there were any wounds. There were none. I wondered if Bay Bay, Winston, or that gunner made it out alive. A flare was shot in the air by the Germans. It lit the area as if it was daylight. I looked next to me and was startled to see a German soldier sitting across from me, pointing a rifle cradle in his left hand. I let out a shout as I pointed my sub machine gun at him. He just sat there, frozen. The light from the flare died down and it was dark again. I took out a small flashlight and flashed it on the German. He was dead, his eyes frozen and lifeless, staring into space. He held the rifle in his left hand, pointing in my direction. There were lightning bolt insignia on his collar and helmet. I slowly crept up next to him. I had read somewhere that a dead person can make a sudden twitch or move, which could cause this German to shoot his rifle. It had something to do with the nervous system or something. I carefully removed his finger from the trigger and tossed the weapon aside. I took a closer look at the corpse. His right hand covered a wound over his belly.

The blood from his wound had dried over his green and gray uniform. He had been shot in the gut and probably knew he was going to die. I saw something in the hand that was covering his injury. Rosary beads. He must have been Catholic. The rosary beads were wrapped around a photo. I removed the beads and looked at the photo. It was of a middle-aged couple with a little girl and a teenaged boy in front of a fireplace. They were standing next to a Christmas tree; the mother and father were laughing, and the two children were smiling. I flashed my flashlight on the dead soldier's face again and realized the boy was him. He was just a boy, younger than me. He might have been, at most, sixteen. I shook my head in sorrow as I compared the photo of the smiling young teenager to this dead soldier. He was so young. He should have been out drinking wine, chasing girls, and celebrating life instead of winding up dead in a ditch in this war-torn country. I wondered if

I was going to turn out like this poor soul. I thought about my mom and dad and wondered if I would ever see them again. I wondered what Lorraine was doing right now. Was she still in the army, or did she get discharged? I thought about the Savoy and Toby's place. I even gave some thought to Gwen.

It was getting darker, and I decided that now was a good time to make my move. I slipped the picture and rosary beads back into the soldier's hand out of respect. I was just about to climb out of the trench, when I heard voices coming from the north side. They were speaking German. I quickly slipped next to the dead German and scooped blood from his wound and smeared it on my face and neck and lay face down, remaining still. A flashlight scanned the area in the trench. They observed the dead German soldier and me. They spoke a few words in German and then hurried off. I was lucky; sometimes they poked a dead enemy soldier with a bayonet to make sure he was dead. I guess they didn't have time to climb down the hole. I waited a few more minutes, until I felt it was safe to come out.

I crawled out of the hole, stood up, then bolted toward the American lines. I slipped and fell. Another flare was shot in the air. I remained perfectly still. The night sky turned to daylight as the flare slowly made its way to the ground on a parachute. When it was dark again, I got up and made my way west. Out of nowhere, two German soldiers appeared in front of me. All of us were startled. They immediately dropped their weapons and raised their hands in the air. "*Nicht schieben! Nicht schieben!*" they shouted. I pointed my grease gun in their direction and directed them to head west. I kept a close eye on them; I had heard stories of German soldiers overpowering their captors by catching them off guard.

"Come on. Move it!" I shouted. "*Schnell! Schnell*! Quick! Quick!" We briskly and quietly moved through the darkness toward the American lines. I heard a shout in front of me.

"Halt! Who goes there?"

"Let me through. I'm Corporal Walter Jenkins of the seven hundred and sixty-first. I have two prisoners with me."

"Advance and be recognized." I came forward, and the sentry shouted, "Halt! Stay right there. I see two Germans." I could hear the click of M1 rifles about to be fired. "I told you," I shouted. "They're prisoners! I'm an American."

"What's the password?" he asked.

"I...I don't know."

"You should know the password, soldier. How do we know you ain't no Kraut?" I stepped into the light with my two prisoners.

"Do I look German to you?" The white soldier looked at me and almost smiled. "Can't say that you do."

CHAPTER 28

A colonel called me into the command tent for a quick briefing. There was a huge map on a display board in front of the tent. There were soldiers manning and monitoring the radios. I could hear typewriters clattering in the corner, and a potbellied stove stood in the middle of the tent, generating heat and comfort. I saluted the colonel, then stood at attention. He returned the salute.

"Stand at ease, corporal," he said. "You did a good job capturing those two German soldiers. They're being interrogated right now. You were deep in enemy territory, so I'm going to need information from you."

I told the colonel as much as I knew. I told him about the Panzer that took us out, about the last position of the 88 mounted on a hilltop, and about the German patrol. After the debriefing, I made my way back to my platoon, where another tank was assigned to me. Bay Bay was missing after our tank exploded, but Winston managed to make it back safely to American lines. The gunner in our tank (I never knew his name) was killed instantly; he was mowed down by German gunfire trying to make it back to the Allied lines.

Winston was sitting on a log, eating out of a can. I couldn't make out what he was eating, but he didn't seem to be enjoying it. I sat down next to him and opened a can of C-rations. I took one bite of what looked and tasted like dog food and put the can aside. I didn't have much of an appetite because of the acrid smell of decaying flesh in the air. Dead German soldiers as well as horses, cows, and other animals were left to rot. The American casualties were immediately taken away, the wounded to field hospitals, the dead to temporary mortuaries. But the German dead were left where they fell, sprawled on the ground.

Another soldier was on top of the tank, cleaning the .50-caliber machine gun. He finished and jumped down from the tank. "My name is Sergeant Tucker," he said.

"I'm Jenkins," I replied.

Tucker was a medium-built, dark-skinned man. He had on his soft army cap, and his sleeves were rolled up to his biceps. He wiped the grease from his hands, then offered a hand to me. We shook.

"Welcome to my tank," he said. "I lost my gunner and loader, so I guess you two guys are going to replace them. What did you do in your tank?"

"I was the driver and Winston over here was the tank commander."

"Well, I don't need a driver, I already have one. You think you can be the gunner?"

"No problem," I replied.

"How did you shoot in training?"

"I was adequate."

Tucker looked down at Winston, who was still eating his meal. "I guess that makes you the loader. You don't mind, do you?"

"Makes no difference to me," he replied.

"So what did you name this tank?" I asked.

"I call her Black Beauty." He looked at me curiously. "So, I hear you were caught behind enemy lines."

"No, not behind enemy lines, but close to it."

"Did you hear about Lieutenant Bates?"

"No."

"He was shot up. They had to evacuate him to the field hospital."

I was instantly concerned. Lieutenant Bates was the one officer I admired and trusted to go into battle with.

"Is he alright?" I asked.

Tucker reached into a cardboard box and pulled out some C-rations. "As far as I know," he said.

"He got his leg shot up pretty bad. Don't know if he'll be able to return to duty."

"Who replaced him?"

"Major Wingo. But when he went up to the battlefield with his Jeep and saw all the commotion, he turned right around and headed in the opposite direction."

"You're kidding me! Major Wingo, the guy who didn't want to be attached to us, saying that we wouldn't fight, he turned chicken?"

Winston started laughing. He laughed so hard he almost fell off the log he was sitting on.

"I guess Wingo was Win-gone," he quipped.

The three of us were laughing up a storm over the irony of it all. Major Wingo hated being attached to an all-black tank battalion, saying that we would be cowards and run off. And at the first sign of battle, he hightailed it to the rear.

"So, who's in command now?" I asked.

"Lieutenant Colonel Hollis Hunt. He's no Lieutenant Bates, but he's better than Wingo," Tucker said.

"What's on the agenda for tomorrow?" I asked.

Tucker finished opening his can of C-rations and placed a spoonful of beans in his mouth. "You know how it is, corporal," he said. "They don't tell us much of anything except when to move and where to go. My guess is, we're gonna resume our offense and attack in the morning against an entrenched German force. So, if I were you, I'd try and get some sleep." At that moment, a figure walked toward us in the distance. Sergeant Tucker stood up and pointed.

"Here he is now. This is the driver of our tank."

To my surprise, it was Charles. It was good to see him. I rushed up and gave him a big bear hug. I guess it might have looked funny, me hugging Charles. But I didn't care if people thought I was gay. It was really good seeing him again. We shook hands.

"Charles, my man, what's happening?"

"You know how it is. I'm keeping my head down and trying to stay alive."

Winston stood, walked over to Charles, and shook his hand vigorously. I guess Winston didn't care if Charles was gay. Something about being in battle changes your perspective on things.

"I see you guys know each other," Tucker said.

"We trained together in the same platoon," I said.

"So you guys are attached to us. What happened to your tank?" Charles asked.

Winston finished the last of his meal and discarded the can.

"We got disabled from hitting a mine, and then a Panzer unit finished the job. Blew our tank to hell," he said.

"Anyone get killed?"

"The gunner," I said. "I forgot his name. I know he was from New Jersey."

"I would rather deal with a Panzer than an eighty-eight," said Tucker. Those suckers can be deadly."

"You're right about that," I said.

"So, what about Bay Bay?" Charles asked. "I heard he was assigned to you guys?"

"He's missing. He'll probably turn up somewhere, I hope. I would hate if anything happened to him. Remember the time we all went to New York and had dinner over my folks' house?"

"Yeah, I remember," Winston said. "Bubba didn't want to eat your mom's curried goat, but once he tasted it, he had two helpings." He took out a filtered cigarette that came with the C-rations. He lit it, inhaled deeply, and then blew out the smoke through his nose and mouth. "Remember we went to Toby's and the Savoy afterward?"

"Yeah, I remember," I replied. "You wound up with some nice-looking lady. What ever happened to her?"

"Nothing. I got her phone number, that's about it."

"What about that white girlfriend of yours in Detroit?" Charles asked.

"That's none of your business," Winston snapped.

Winston didn't like talking about his white girlfriend much. In those days, you didn't see many interracial relationships. I got a glimpse of her from a picture she sent him; she wasn't a bad looking woman. I guess Charles brought her up to make a point about interracial dating and homosexual dating.

"So have you heard from Tank?" I asked, quickly changing the subject.

"I saw him the other day," Charles said. "He' attached over at Able Company. I think he said he was an assistant driver."

"When there's a lull in the fighting, we should all hook up," I said.

"Yeah, we should all hook up and swap war stories. I heard about those two Krauts you captured," Winston said.

"You know, for the life of me I can't figure out why those two Krauts gave up. There were two of them and one of me. They could have easily overpowered me."

"I guess they wanted to sit out the rest of the war in a prison camp. Can't say that I blame them," Winston said.

I looked at Winston and realized that all the bluster and glory he had earlier was gone. He just wanted to survive the war like the rest of us. The difference between him and me was that I knew what to expect from the beginning. At that point, Sergeant Tucker poked his head out of the tank's hatch.

I know it's tough, but you guys should grab what sleep you can get. It's gonna be a busy day tomorrow," he said.

We took his advice and set up our pup tents. Tucker stayed inside the tank by himself. I lay in my tent in my sleeping bag, nervously thinking about the outcome the following day. I could have slept in the tank, but I preferred to sleep outside. When it got cold, the tank was like a refrigerator. I slid into the sleeping bag under my small tent and tried to get what little sleep I could. It was hard to get a good night's sleep out there, knowing that the next day you'll be going into battle. I remembered what my father's friend Mr. Francis had told me back in New York about being in battle and that I should keep my head down. But that was the First World War; it was trench warfare, one gigantic stalemate. Everyone stayed in their trenches lobbing bombs at each other, blowing each other to bits. But this war was different, a lighting war. The Germans called it Blitzkrieg, which involved sophisticated tanks and airplanes. You had to do more than keeping your head down to survive. I lay in my sleeping bag, half my body out of my pup tent, looking up at the sky. The moon peeked through the overcast clouds and I marveled at the beauty of it all, the moon against the bright and spectacular stars, and wondered if the Germans were admiring the same moon. Here we are, God's creatures, and we are inflicting so much pain and anguish on each other. I lay on my back looking at the stars and wondered if this insane war would ever end.

CHAPTER 29

Wake-up time was 5:00 am. I got very little sleep, if you want to call it that. Light snow had fallen during the night, leaving some snow on my tent and at the edge of my sleeping bag. I woke up with my hands feeling numb and my feet freezing. Sergeants went around to each tank and pup tent, getting us up and preparing us for battle. There were heated metal barrels filled with water and eggs. The cooks were preparing a meal of hard-boiled eggs with creamed chipped beef and toast. I couldn't help but notice that most of the cooks were black. They looked at us with wonderment and pride, seeing black tankers in the chow line. We ate quickly so the food wouldn't get cold in the freezing temperature. I ate some of my breakfast but couldn't finish it. I didn't have much of an appetite due to nervousness.

After breakfast, we went to our respective tanks. Sergeant Tucker was already greasing the .50- caliber machine gun, something he always seemed to be doing. Winston was checking the tracks on the tank, clearing all the mud and muck they had collected the previous day. Revving engines could be heard in the distance, like race cars at the Indy 500. Charles sat behind the controls of the tank. I went to my station behind the 75-mm cannon. Winston sat beside the shelves stacked with heavy explosives, ready to load when told. I looked at the wall and realized the picture of Billie Holiday was gone, incinerated in the Harlem Raiders, the previous tank. I checked and rechecked the cannon, making sure it was clear of dirt and debris. I wouldn't want to have my cannon backfire.

After checking our equipment, we drove to the gas line and waited our turn behind other tanks. After we gassed up our war machines, an infantry sergeant shouted, "Are you ready?" Tucker gave him the thumbs up, and the sergeant walked in front of the tank, guiding us onto the main road. We rendezvoused in an open field not far from camp, where another meeting was held, and final instructions were given to the tank commanders. Tucker came back from the meeting and boarded the tank. He slid down the turret and placed his tank helmet on his head. A speaker was attached to the helmets that also served as a radio. He flipped the switch and turned up the volume on the intercom so we could hear his instructions. The rest of us put on our tank helmets so we could hear him. His helmet radio also allowed him to hear from other tanks in the field.

"All right, Charles, I want you to follow that lead tank," he said. "We're gonna cover the right flank of the main thrust. So, keep your eyes peeled, men. We don't want the Jerries outflanking us." We followed the lead tank north, traveling slowly at about fifteen miles per hour, looking for any sign of German activity. "Easy now, Charles. Keep your eyes peeled." Every now and then, Tucker would lift his head from the turret and scan the area with his binoculars for a brief minute or two, wary of German snipers in the area.

The tanks continued their slow journey north. The white infantry men were walking in two columns, one on each side. Some of them were behind us, thinking that the tanks would give them protection. They were wrong about that. A tank was the first thing the Jerries would want to take out with their powerful 88-mm anti-tank weapons or Panzerfausts, German bazookas. The deadly shrapnel and debris would cause heavy casualties if the infantry men followed too closely.

It was a cold and muddy autumn morning. The snow dusting was only a prelude to the winter months ahead. Why don't the Germans just give up? I thought. Why do they want to carry on this fight, making life miserable for them and us? It was clear that they were going to lose the war. The Russians were winning battle after battle, pushing west; the Allied forces were pushing east, liberating every city and town in their path. Why are they so fanatical, why are they causing so much pain for everyone? The Sherman tanks traveled in single formation about thirty feet apart.

A lieutenant who was monitoring us pulled up in a Jeep and gave the command for all tanks to stop. He then directed one tank to back up into a deserted barn, another behind a haystack, and another on a hilltop. The white infantry soldiers in the area weren't happy to see that we were black, but were happy tanks were there to back them up.

"I want tanks thirty-four and forty-two to go up that ridge and check it out," the lieutenant said over the radio.

We were tank thirty-four. We turned and headed north; with tank forty-two about thirty yards beside us. A platoon of infantry men was behind each tank. We carefully drove our tanks up toward the ridge. There was a group of infantry engineers already ahead of us, checking for mine fields.

"Easy now," said Tucker. "Watch that right flank."

My eye was pressed hard against the periscope. My hands, trembling and sweaty, were on the trigger of the cannon, ready to fire on command. We began to hear heavy fighting in the distance just west of us. It looked like the main thrust was beginning their attack. Tucker gave the order to load the cannon. Winston reached for the rack on the turret floor, grabbed a heavy explosive, and slammed it in the breech. I waited for the command to fire, but at what? I didn't see anything. Suddenly, smoke bombs exploded in front of us about a hundred meters away. The Germans were either trying to conceal their movements or marking the spot for artillery fire. Charles slowly steered the tank closer to the line of smoke. When a 78-mm barrel from a tank peered through the smoke ahead of us, Charles pulled back on both levers and our tank jolted to a halt. We were face to- face with the dreaded German Panzer tank. The Panzer was far more superior to our Sherman tank in fire power and durability.

We were trained not to go one-on-one with the Panzer, but to outmaneuver or overwhelm it. We had more tanks than the Germans, and while the Panzer had more fire-power and stronger armor, it was difficult to maintain. The Sherman tank, on the other hand, had a simpler design. If there was a problem with a track or the engine, it was easier to fix. The Panzer was a more complicated war machine. It took time to fix whatever problem it might have.

Charles quickly threw the tank in reverse and gunned it backward before the Panzer could get a bead on us. The Sherman tank to the right of us fired a missile. The round bounced off the front end. The Panzer turned its attention to the tank and fired a deadly round, hitting the right side of the Sherman tank. It was a direct hit; the missile struck the right-side track, disabling the tank. The Panzer had made an error. Instead of dealing with us, it went for the Sherman tank next to us. By swinging the cannon around, it exposed its left side, which is the most vulnerable spot on a Panzer.

Without waiting for the order to fire, I pulled the trigger and fired a round. Sergeant Tucker looked at me surprised that I didn't wait for his command. The cannon recoiled, ejecting the shell. It was a direct hit. Burning steel and metal flew in the air. Shadowy figures began bailing out of the Panzer and hightailing it to the rear. Some were mowed down by American infantry soldiers. The remaining Germans in the blazing tank came out. One was waving a white flag; the others had their hands raised in the air, shouting, "*Nicht scheiben! Nicht scheiben!*" They were immediately taken prisoner and led away. Winston threw another round in the chamber. I was about to fire another round to finish off the crippled tank, but Tucker told me to hold my fire.

The Sherman tank next to us sustained heavy damage, but no loss of human life. We continued eastward with Tucker observing the front line with his binoculars. The order was given over the radio to hold our position. Later, other tanks from our rear reinforced us. The infantry soldiers cautiously worked their way in front of us, checking for mines and tank traps.

"That was a gutsy move on your part, Jenkins, firing without my authorization," Tucker said.

"I saw an opening and I took advantage of it," I said.

"It doesn't matter, there's certain procedures that must be followed when you're out here. I'm the tank commander and you wait for my order to fire, understood?" I nodded my head. "I'm not going to make an issue out of it, because you were lucky. We got good results. But the next time this happens, I'm going to take action."

Again, I nodded my head. What else could I do? He did outrank me. I didn't take him seriously though. What could he do, reprimand me for destroying a German Panzer and assisting in the capture of German soldiers? Sometimes you have to use initiative when you're in battle. Winston smiled, and Charles gave me the thumbs up.

The American soldiers in the main thrust met heavy casualties. The Germans' resistance was tough. The Americans paid dearly for the land they managed to occupy. On the right flank, where I was, we met little resistance. We destroyed two Panzer tanks and captured about twenty German soldiers. We came upon a town named Morville. We were ordered to hold our position on the outskirts of town until reinforcements arrived. The 458th arrived with their lighter tanks and were ordered to get as close to the town as possible and bring back information about the position of the enemy's guns and equipment. As the light tanks rattled toward the town, I saw Bubba standing out of the hatch behind a .60-calber machine gun. They were sending him on a dangerous recon mission, and although we had that bitter fight back in England, I hoped that he would pull out of this alive.

CHAPTER 30

We were still lined up on the outskirts of the town of Morville. Four more tanks from the 761st lined up next to us to give support to the 26th Infantry Division, which was going into town. The 458th was at the entrance and received no enemy fire. The soldiers and engineers cautiously worked their way into town, checking each building and clearing the area of mines or tank traps. Winston leaned forward and revealed some bad news. Bay Bay had been found dead in a ditch, shot several times in the stomach. All my hopes that he survived the attack on our tank, the Harlem Raiders, were dashed.

"Are you sure it was him?" I asked.

Winston nodded his head. "A friend over in Alpha Company confirmed it. He must have run in the wrong direction like you did only he ran directly behind enemy lines."

Suddenly there was an explosion and gunfire coming from the town. I looked in the periscope and saw a tank on fire and several infantry soldiers being mowed down by machine gunfire. Tucker lowered his head from the turret and gave the order to move out. We began rolling down the path toward the town, behind the lead tank. There was no time to mourn Bay Bay's death. We were given orders to support the infantry, who were pinned down. Some of the soldiers were already fleeing the town, carrying their wounded. We lined up at the entrance of the town and all four tanks laid a heavy barrage of motor fire. We blew up buildings suspected of harboring German snipers, machine-gun nests, and anti-tank weapons.

Winston slammed a round into the chamber, and Tucker gave me the order to shoot at a church steeple. It seemed sacrilegious to me and I hesitated at first, but I fired. German snipers were known for hiding in church steeples, waiting for an opportunity to shoot at any unsuspecting soldier. The steeple exploded and remnants fell to the ground, leaving a pile of rubble. We continued firing upon the village, leaving more piles of trash and debris. Flames flickered out of store front windows, and the stench of burning flesh could be smelled in the air. We began to drive into town single file; there was a tank ahead of us and two behind us.

Suddenly there was another tremendous explosion in front of us, and in an instant the tank ahead of us was engulfed in flames. Soldiers consumed by fire were jumping out of the turret and hatch. Only to be cut down by German machine gunfire. We heard another explosion as the last tank was hit. That tank was a burning inferno. The soldiers inside didn't even have time to try to escape; they were cremated. Both tanks had been hit by the deadly 88-mm. The 88 was originally built to shoot down aircraft, it was later used as an anti-tank weapon, and it was lethal. Tucker spotted where the 88 was located and ordered me to swing the cannon forty degrees to the left. Winston slammed a motor into the breech. I fired. Tucker looked through his binoculars. "You almost had him," he said. Two more degrees to the left."

I adjusted the cannon and as soon as Winston threw another motor in the chamber, I fired another round. It was a direct hit. We could see shadowy figures fleeing the scene and seeking shelter. The Germans had us boxed in. The last tank and the tank in front of us were burning wrecks. The tank directly behind us was still intact; they fired a few more rounds at the disabled 88 to make sure it was destroyed. We were in a dangerous crossfire. The Germans had us in their sights, some of them entrenched in the rubble and abandoned buildings. Charles was frantically trying to work his way around the destroyed tank in front of us, when an enemy soldier appeared at a second-floor window of an apartment building with a Panzerfaust and fired. The missile hit our tracks, damaging the undercarriage and volute springs. The tank behind us immediately swung its cannon around and fired at the building. Smoldering rocks and debris fell to the pavement below. Bullets from machine-gun fire were pinging on both tanks. The left track was damaged but still operational. Charles gunned the gas pedal and tried to drive around the damaged tank, but the Germans fired another Panzerfaust in the opposite direction, damaging the right track.

With only my right hand on the .50-caliber, I remained stooped down in the turret and shot in the direction where the last missile was fired. Both tracks were severely damaged, but the tank managed to move at a slow pace. We could hear voices on the radio from different sources. One message was from a captain in the 761st.

"We can see you guys are having trouble in there. Are there any casualties?" he asked.

"The lead tank and the last tank are gone, sir. Everyone in both tanks is dead," Tucker said.

"Stay hunkered in. Reinforcements are on the way, but they're encountering heavy resistance."

"Can you give us an idea of when they'll get here, sir? It's really hot down here. They got us pinned down in both directions."

"Just keep your heads down."

The tank behind us came in over the radio. "Can you guys work your way to that building to the left?"

Tucker and I checked our periscope and saw a building that looked to be an abandoned warehouse. "I don't know, it looks like there could be Krauts in there," Tucker said.

"Just see if you can work your way over there. We'll keep you covered."

Charles pulled hard on the left lever. The tank bumped and rattled and slowly crept toward our destination when Tucker saw something through his periscope. "Hold up Charles. What's that over there?"

I checked my scope and saw smoke billowing in the distance. "That looks like a tank. Is it one of ours?"

"Yeah, it looks like one of those light weights that were sent on that recon mission. Looks like they're disabled and pinned down," Tucker said.

We didn't know exactly how far that tank was from us. Looking through the periscope in a tank distorts your peripheral vision. We tried to reach the crippled tank by radio, but there was no response.

"You think you can drive over there, Charles, and see if there are any survivors?" Tucker asked.

"I don't know, Sarge. These tracks are pretty much damaged, but I'll give it a shot."

Charles pressed on the gas pedal and drove the tank. As we got closer, we could make out two white infantry men lying at the bottom of the tank, seeking shelter. There was no way to communicate with them or anybody inside the tank. Another round from a Panzerfaust slammed into our tank, hitting the right track, further damaging the belt and wheels. The Sherman tank came to an abrupt halt.

Charles gave it gas, but it wouldn't budge. The tank behind us retaliated by shooting a high explosive shell at the last position where the enemy's missile had come from, blowing a gigantic hole in a building that looked to have been a drug store. Charles gunned the engine, but the tank was immobilized; it wouldn't move an inch.

"I'm afraid were stuck here, Sarge," Charles said.

Tucker again tried to gain contact with the disabled light tank, but still there was no response. Incoming bullets and motor shells were getting intense. It looked like the Germans were concentrating their fire power on us.

"We're sitting ducks out here," Winston shouted.

"We would be if they had another eighty-eight around," Tucker said.

"What makes you think they don't?" I asked.

"I think the one we took out was the only one they had. If they did have another one, we would have had a taste of it by now."

"How can you be so sure?" Winston asked.

"I can't, it's just a gut feeling."

A voice came over the radio. Tucker adjusted his microphone to make out who it was. It was the tank directly behind us. "I thought I told you guys to go over to the building back there for cover."

"We spotted a disabled tank. It's one of ours. There's two GI's underneath it and we don't know if anybody's inside. How about giving us some cover while we check it out," Tucker said.

"You sure you want to do that? It's pretty hot out here."

"I've got to try something. We just can't leave those guys like that," Tucker said.

Another Panzerfaust was fired in our direction, missing our tank completely. The Sherman tank behind us swung its 75-mm gun around and fired a missile in the direction of the muzzled fire. An explosion ripped apart the building, causing the front structure to collapse, leaving a pile of rubble on the ground. The tank then reversed its engine to go on the offense, when the driver backed into a tank trap, a hole in the ground filled with cranes and stones, which left the tank immobile. The tank tipped at an angle, exposing the bottom. It was the most vulnerable spot on a Sherman tank and an easy target. A hit from a Panzerfaust would cause serious damage. The cannons were in an upward position so they couldn't be used against the enemy. I saw a German soldier in the open with a Panzerfaust slung on his shoulder taking aim at the immobilized Sherman tank. I immediately opened the hatch, exposing myself to enemy gunfire, and began firing the .50-caliber machine gun toward him. He ran for shelter behind a pile of rubble, which gave the soldiers in the tank time to evacuate and seek cover.

Bullets pinged around me as I ducked back down the hatch. Tucker looked through the periscope and saw the crew in the disabled tank behind us; they escaped through the bottom hatch and turret and remained next to the tank in the anti-tank ditch. We were pinned down pretty good. It was only a matter of time before the Germans would bring up the heavy artillery. Charles looked through his scope and observed the two Americans soldiers lying underneath the damaged tank ahead of us.

"I'm going to make a dash for that tank," he said.

"Don't be a fool!" I shouted, trying to talk over the incoming gunfire. "They'll cut you to pieces!"

"I've got to find out if anyone is inside that tank. Cover me." Before Tucker or I could stop him, Charles opened the bottom hatch and crawled up to the front.

"What are we going to do?" I asked.

"Nothing we can do but give him cover," Tucker said. "You cover the north side, I'll take the south."

I mounted the .50-caliber. Tucker mounted the .60-caliber. Winston threw a high explosive into the chamber, then went to the gunner position.

"All right. Let's wait until he makes a break for it," Tucker shouted.

Charles got up from under the tank and sprinted toward the crippled tank. I fired the .50caliber. Tucker fired his weapon, while Winston fired the cannon at the building we believed was harboring the machine-gun nest. Debris and rubble flew from the building. With bullets exploding around him, Charles dove underneath the disabled tank. Tucker and I ducked back into the safety of our tank. We didn't want to be exposed in the open too long. I looked through the driver's periscope and saw Charles talking to the infantry soldiers. He then banged his fist against the bottom hatch, and to my surprise, the hatch opened.

There was somebody inside, but who? There was still heavy traffic on the radio. All soldiers on the battlefield were talking at once. The 761st was still trying to break through the stubborn German line surrounding the town. The Twenty-Sixth Infantry was pinned down south of us. They were requesting artillery fire. Then Charles voice came over the radio.

"I've got one man alive here. It's Bubba. He's wounded," he said.

"How bad is he?" Tucker asked. "Can you move him?"

"I'm afraid not. His legs are shot up pretty bad. I'm going to apply some first aid."

"How are the soldiers under the tank?"

"They're okay."

"Tell them that we're gonna give them cover, to make a break for that anti-tank ditch behind us.

Some of our boys are over there, and they seem to be dug in."

"I don't know about that," Charles responded. "It's quite a distance; they'll get cut down for sure."

Tucker looked at Winston and me. "How much ammo do we have left?" he asked.

We made a quick inventory of our ordnance while Tucker maintained radio communication. We had three high explosives, six smoke bombs, and three cases of .50 and .60-caliber bullets. We had four clips for the .45 and six magazines for the grease gun. Tucker adjusted the frequency on the radio.

"Listen up, Charles," Tucker said over the radio. "I want you and the other soldiers to make a break for that ditch behind us. We're gonna fire smoke bombs to give you cover."

"What about Bubba?" Charles asked.

"Can you move him?"

"Not the way his legs are. I cleaned his wounds the best I could, and I have him sedated with morphine."

"Leave him there for now. The Germans will think the tank is empty and will concentrate on us."

"Are you sure that's what you want to do?"

"Just do it! When you see the smoke, make a break for it."

I gripped Tucker's elbow firmly. "You just can't leave him there like that," I said.

"I have no other choice. He'll be safe in there as long as the Krauts think it's empty. Besides, I'm responsible for the rest of you guys. Now prepare to fire that cannon."

Winston handed me a shell, and I quickly slammed it into the breech and waited for the command to fire. Tucker looked through the periscope, sweat dripping from his forehead. "Fire!" he shouted.

I pulled the trigger, and the cannon fired a round. Smoke exploded in front of us. Winston slammed another shell in the chamber and fired again. Lines of smoke spread through the air as the Germans fired their weapon blindly in our direction. The white infantry soldiers got out from underneath the tank and dashed toward the trench. Tucker and I also sprinted to the tank at the rear of our position. We jumped into the anti-tank ditch, joining the other soldiers. The commander of the crippled tank was a staff sergeant, the same rank as Tucker. He was a tall lanky fellow with a fuzzy mustache. He was about forty, light-skinned, with a flat nose. It looked like his nose had been broken a few times; he might have been a boxer.

"You guys all right?" Tucker asked.

"We're fine," the light-skinned sergeant answered. "The tank ain't damaged, just can't get it out of this damned hole."

Tucker whipped out his binoculars and observed the area. "There's a warehouse across the street. I don't see any activity in there, maybe we can make it across."

The light- skinned sergeant surveyed the warehouse with his binoculars. "I think we should just dig in here and wait for reinforcements."

I couldn't help but think about Bubba alone in that tank. There was a brief lull in the fighting and a chance to take advantage of it. "I'm gonna work my way to Bubba's tank and pull him out," I said.

"You'll do nothing of the sort!" Tucker shouted. "As soon as the smoke clears, the Germans will continue hammering us. We dig in here and wait for reinforcements."

"There's no telling how long it will take," I retorted. "He's dying in there while we're out here twiddling our thumbs."

"If you got a wounded man in there, maybe we should try to do something," the light- skinned sergeant said.

Before Tucker could answer, a soldier pointed in the air and asked, "Are those birds up there?" We all looked up to what appeared to be birds flying; it was somewhat eerie seeing birds in the sky. I had never seen birds flying in the middle of a war zone, especially when the battle had been going on for several hours. The birds were getting larger when I realized they weren't birds, but incoming shells. "In coming!" I shouted. Everyone hustled out of the ditch.

Shells were coming down in a line, methodically eliminating each spot. Tucker somehow got entangled in a gun belt. Just as he managed to untangle his foot, a shell came crashing on him. His body parts flew in different directions. The blast knocked me to the ground. Tucker's dismembered arm fell next to me. I didn't have time to mull over the grisly scene. Bullets were rattling around me, and the Germans were cutting us down as we came out of the trench. I heard someone shout my name, and I realized some of the men had managed to make it across to the warehouse.

As I desperately crawled towards the safety of the warehouse, I noticed one of the white infantry soldiers lying dead on the ground, cut down by enemy gunfire. A shell erupted next to him. Shrapnel shredded his body, splattering his blood on my face. Winston and the other soldiers were desperately gesturing for me to crawl faster. I frantically slithered through the snow and ice while bullets whizzed over me like angry bees. My arms were bruised and bleeding as I kept my body as close to the ground as possible. The snow was wet and cold, but I kept my head buried, praying that I would make it out alive. For some reason, there was a brief pause in the bullets exploding around me. I got up and sprinted as fast as I could. I jumped through the open door, falling on the ground. The light-skinned sergeant slammed the door behind me.

"You're lucky you made it, son," he said. "If it wasn't for that soldier in that tank giving you cover, you would have been a goner."

"What soldier?" I asked. The sergeant gave me his binoculars. I took them and cautiously crept to the window. I saw Charles manning a .60-caliber machine gun in the disabled tank, shooting at the enemy positions. "I thought everyone evacuated," I said.

"They were supposed to, I guess he disobeyed orders and stayed behind."

There were three dead German solders spread across the room. They looked to have been caught in an explosion, probably hit by shrapnel from our tanks. Just then, a white infantry soldier and a black soldier with a bandolier slung over his shoulder appeared on the top stairwell of the warehouse. The white soldier had his M1 rifle cradle in his hands. He did not have his helmet on, and his face and hair were wet from either snow or sweat. The black soldier had his grease gun in tow and his tank helmet on. A German soldier was in front of him with his hands held high.

"We found this one hiding upstairs," the white soldier said, and we have a wounded German upstairs. Other than that, everything seems to be clear." The German prisoner was dirty and nervous. His hands were trembling as he held them high in the air.

"Tie that one up, and you two stay upstairs," the light-skinned sergeant said. "Report any movements you see outside to me. This is a better place than any to hole up and wait for reinforcements. How bad is the wounded German?"

"I don't know," the black soldier said. He's delirious and seems to be in a lot of pain."

"Give him one shot of morphine and that's all. I don't want you wasting what little medicine we have on the enemy."

"What about Charles? He can't last in that tank by himself," I said.

"He was ordered to leave and he chose to stay. It's all on him now."

I once again checked on Charles through the binoculars and saw him firing away in the enemy's direction. "I'm going in there," I said.

The light-skinned sergeant looked at me, startled. "Are you crazy, man?" he said. "You're lucky to have survived that last encounter. You cheated death once, now you want to dance with the devil again. Don't push your luck, son. It's not worth it."

"Somebody has to help him man that fifty, Sarge. He can't hold them off with that sixty alone." I looked through the spy glass again and noticed three German soldiers inching their way up to the crippled tank. The light-skinned sergeant observed the enemy's line through his binoculars while I continued to plead my case. "It's only a matter of time before they knock off that tank, then they'll concentrate on us," I said. "And there's no telling when reinforcements will get here."

"I'm not partial to sending a man to his death, but if that's what you want to do…" the light skinned sergeant said.

"It's not what I want to do. I have to do it."

I took off my pack, placed my grease gun aside, and then took off my holster with the .45 pistol. I'd be able to run faster without all that equipment, and the tank had plenty of fire power I could use. There was a temporary lull in the fighting. I opened the door and made a dash for the tank. Bullets whizzed through the air as I ran as fast as could to the disabled tank. A bullet caught me in the leg just as I leaped under the tank. Charles opened the bottom hatch and assisted me inside.

"What are you doing here?" he asked.

"I figured you might need a hand."

"You're one crazy Negro, you know that? You should have stayed behind." He looked at my leg and noticed the wound. "Hey man, you're bleeding all over the place. Sit down."

I sat down while he wrapped a tourniquet around the wound to contain the bleeding. Then he quickly went to the turret and proceeded firing the .60-caliber. I got up and took a belt of bullets from a crate. I lifted the lid of the .50-caliber machine gun and placed the bullets inside. I looked through the periscope and saw smoke from a weapon coming from the second-floor window across the street. I cocked the level at the side of the .50 and began shooting a deadly stream of tracer fire at the enemy's line. The Germans who were working their way up to our tank ran for cover behind piles of rubble. My heart was pounding, and although it was cold, I was sweating profusely. I saw a German soldier with a Panzerfaust. He was about to fire, but I laid some heavy fire on him and he ducked behind the safety of a building. The sun had reached its full zenith and the battle was still going on. There was no sign of reinforcements, and the Germans seemed to have plenty of fight left in them. I saw Bubba on the floor. He was lapsing in and out of consciousness and was delirious. I found a blanket in a discarded pack and covered him. I elevated his legs to prevent him from going into shock. I then went back and resumed my post behind the .50-caliber machine gun.

Charles was covering the left side with his .60 and I was covering the right. If the enemy decided to try to flank us from the rear, the guys in the warehouse could try to hold them back. But how much longer can this go on, I thought.

"How much ammo you have left?" Charles asked.

"Two crates," I said.

"I have one box left. We're gonna have to conserve our fire power. Shoot only at an open target."

I stopped firing my weapon and looked carefully for an open target. A German soldier stepped from behind a pile of rubble with a Panzerfaust mounted on his shoulder. Before we could react, he fired. The deadly missile struck the center of the tank, knocking us both to the floor. The missile did not penetrate but caused further damage to the front end. We immediately got back on our feet and began firing our weapons. A bullet jammed in my machine gun. I lifted the lid and ejected the jammed bullet. I realigned the belt, being careful not to touch the hot barrel. I slammed the lid shut and began firing at anything that moved.

"I don't know how much longer we can keep this up, Charles," I shouted. There was no response.

"Charles?"

I looked to my left, and Charles was not there. I looked on the floor and saw him sprawled face down in a pool of blood. I instantly dropped down next to him and rolled him over. He was dead, with a giant hole in the middle of his face, and some bullet holes across his chest. I cradled him in my arms and wept.

CHAPTER 31

I don't know how long I nestled Charles in my arms. A German soldier tossed a grenade into the tank. I instantaneously leaped to the grenade and threw it back outside. It was just in the nick of time. The explosion could be heard outside. I took one more look at Charles's lifeless body and something came over me, I don't know what it was, anger, rage, or hopelessness. I stood up in the turret of the tank, exposing myself to enemy gunfire. I began firing the .50-caliber, ripping away at the enemy's position. I spotted some Germans retreating from their position in front of the tank. I gunned them down. The German soldier who was behind the pile of rubble attempted again to fire his Panzerfaust. I cut him down with a stream of bullets. He fell backward, his Panzerfaust firing a missile harmlessly in the air, striking a building across the street.

Bullets rattled over my head and in front of the tank, but I relentlessly fired my weapon. The machine gun clicked. I was out of bullets. I quickly went to the crate and got another belt of bullets, reloaded, and began firing. I caught a bullet in the upper part of my chest. I fell to the steel floor but sprang back up to my feet and kept firing. Another bullet ripped into my lower right side. I was disoriented for a moment and fell to the floor once more. I gathered myself together and got back up on my feet. I spotted a German soldier creeping up to the tank with a hand grenade. I immediately shot him down. The hand grenade fell next to him and exploded.

Bullets were popping and snapping in front of me and above me on the open hatch. I did not seek cover, and I don't know why I left myself open to enemy gunfire. I kept firing my .50-caliber machine gun at the German lines, screaming every obscenity that came to mind, venting my anger and frustration at the stubborn German resistance. I thought of Charles, Tucker, and Bay Bay as I hammered away at the enemy's position. I heard the rattling sound of tank tracks behind me. I turned around and saw some tanks from the 761st making their way through. White infantry soldiers were at the side, clearing buildings of machine-gun nests and snipers. Reinforcements were here! They had finally broken through the lines.

The Germans began fleeing from their entrenched positions, running from the oncoming

American juggernaut. The tanks began laying an onslaught of heavy explosives on the town, leveling every building and pile of rubble suspected of harboring enemy soldiers. A tank to my left fired a round into a building where a machine-gun nest was strategically placed in the basement, its barrel sticking out from the bottom window surrounded by sandbags. The complex erupted from the high explosive. The machine-gun nest disappeared in the collapsing building, leaving a trail of dust and rubble. I feverishly continued firing my weapon. I saw a German soldier running away to my right. I swung my .50-caliber around and aimed at the fleeing soldier. I fired a blast. His upper torso ripped away from his legs. His legs were still running before collapsing about twenty feet. I was stunned by the gruesome sight and stopped firing.

A white infantry soldier saw what happened. "That Kraut didn't know if he was coming or going," he quipped to his buddy.

I leaned to the side of the tank and vomited.

CHAPTER 32

The Sherman tanks continued laying a heavy barrage on the town, clearing it of any remaining German resistance. American infantry soldiers went from building to building, eliminating any hint of enemy presence. Most of the town was destroyed. Remnants of old buildings that had stood for centuries were now piles of rubble. Soot and ashes littered the town; plumes of smoke could be seen for miles around the countryside. The smell of smoke drifted in the air, a reminder of the devastating battle that had taken place. Mangled German corpses could be seen in the middle of the streets. The American dead were quickly whisked away to the rear of the Allied lines, to a temporary mortuary. I stood behind the .50 caliber machine gun, my fingers still frozen on the trigger. Some medics boarded the tank and evacuated Bubba to the rear, to a medical facility.

Winston strolled up to me with his grease gun in hand. "You okay?" he asked. I said nothing, my eyes fixed on the German soldier I had just ripped apart with my machine gun. The light-skinned sergeant entered the tank and stood behind Winston.

"That was quite a show you put on out there young man," he said. "What's your name?" I remained silent. I was still in a state of shock. "I'm going to recommend a medal," he said.

Winston gave me a closer look. "Are you okay, Walter?" he asked again. He snapped his fingers in front of my face; he looked down and noticed blood seeping from my side. Everything started spinning, and the next thing I knew, my face was kissing the steel floor of the tank. Just before I blacked out, I heard Winston shouting for a medic. I felt myself drifting off into a blackened vortex of infinity.

I opened my eyes and saw the blue sky and realized I was on a stretcher strapped to the hood of a Jeep. I blacked out again and heard random sounds, and saw lights going and coming. Again, there was a long silence, followed by voices and sounds. I smelled the strange smell of ether and methanol. I opened my eyes and saw a blurred vision of a white woman in a white uniform and nurse's cap, looking down on me.

"You're finally awake. How you feeling, soldier?" she asked. I wanted to speak, but my throat was dry and hoarse. I could only manage a faint whisper. "Don't try to speak," she said. "Save your strength. The doctor will be here to speak to you in a moment. You want something to drink?" I nodded my head, and she disappeared from the room.

I looked around at my surroundings and noticed two more patients in the room with me. One was a white GI who seemed to be in a coma. The other was wrapped in bandages from his head down to his shoulders. I couldn't tell what race he was. I had an IV attached to my arm and some type of tube placed inside the wound on my right side. I turned my head and saw a window to my left. It appeared to be nighttime, it was dark outside. The bed was hot, and I shifted my feet and felt the pain in my leg. The nurse returned with a paper cup filled with ice and water, and a straw sticking up in the middle. She placed the straw in my mouth, and I gingerly sipped. I lay back in the bed and closed my eyes. When I opened my eyes again, it was daylight.

A thin doctor with jet-black hair with strands of gray on top approached my bedside. He was slightly tanned, and I wondered where he got the tan from here in France. He must have just come from the States, I thought, California or maybe Florida. He checked my pulse, then went over my chest with his stethoscope, moving it up and down, checking my heartbeat.

"My name is Epstein," he said gently. "When you were brought in, you were close to death. You're a lucky man." Once again, I tried to speak, but could only manage a whisper. "Don't speak, just listen. The bullet that hit your leg damaged the bone, and the bullet that hit your chest went clean through. No vital parts were damaged, so you are lucky in that sense. You lost a lot of blood. It was cold outside, and that managed to slow the bleeding, otherwise you would have bled to death."

"What concerns me is the bullet that went into your right side next to your stomach. It went in at an angle and is still wedge in there, close to your spinal cord; it could paralyze you for life. We're going to operate as soon as you feel strong enough. It's a delicate procedure, but according to your x-rays, we should be able to pull it off. We're going to give you soft foods and wait for your strength to build, then we're going to take it from there. Any questions?"

I shook my head, and Epstein hurried off to service other soldiers. I lay on the hospital bed feeling depressed. I could be paralyzed for life. I was twenty-three years old and could wind up in some nursing home being waited on hand and foot. I wouldn't be able to bathe myself, brush my teeth, or tie my shoes. It was too depressing to even think about. I drifted off again, and when I woke up, there was a black nurse standing over me. She was dark-skinned, with a wide gap between her front teeth. Her hair was processed and rolled in a tight bun. She had a pan with soapy water and a sponge at the side.

"I'm going to give you a sponge bath. You feel up to it?" she asked in an authoritarian voice.

I nodded my head, and she proceeded to partially undress me. She began washing down my chest, arms, and private parts. While she was bathing me, she was complaining.

"Those damn nurses. Don't want to bathe a colored man. They say they never gave a Negro a bath before and don't know how; I told them you bathe a black man like anyone else. They think they're too good to bathe you. They need to get off their high and mighty lily-white asses and do their job." She gave me a good washing, then dried me. She buttoned up my clothes and started walking toward the door, still venting her frustration. "I don't care what color you are, "she said. "I bathe everyone. Those lily-white nurses can kiss my black ass."

She walked out the door and down the hallway, I wondered if she was always this bitter or if those nurses who always seemed so nice were complaining about me. The washing I received made me feel fresh and clean. I hadn't had a good bath in about a month. Being on the battlefield, you have to forget such luxuries.

CHAPTER 33

I don't know how long I was there, but I started to feel a little stronger. I could sit up without help. They removed the IV and started me on soft foods: soup, applesauce, and pudding. What I would have given for a steak with rice. Epstein made his way into the room.

"I see you can sit up by yourself," he said "I would advise you not to. That bullet is still wedged close to your spine, and any movement of that bullet could paralyze you."

"I'll be careful, sir." He was a Major, and I wasn't sure if I should address him as "doctor" or "sir." I called him "sir "to be on the safe side. He grabbed a stool and sat on it next to my bedside.

"I don't want you eating anything after ten o' clock," he said. "You're scheduled for surgery tomorrow. We're going to attempt to get that bullet out."

"What are my chances of not being paralyzed, sir?"

"I don't like giving percentages, but like I told you before, according to the x-rays I'm confident that I'll be able to pull this off." He stood from the stool, checked the charts, then hurried off.

Early the next morning, the black nurse was back, and all that bitterness she was harboring a few days earlier seemed to have melted away. She was a little more pleasant. She asked me where I was from, and I told her. She told me she was from Baltimore and was planning to visit Harlem. I had pre-surgery jitters, and I guess she was trying to relax me with conversation. She finished prepping me, and I was rolled into a large room where doctors were preforming surgery on other wounded soldiers who had been brought in from the front lines. I tried to get a better look at my surroundings, but someone placed a gas mask over my face. Before I knew it, I blacked out.

I woke up to find myself in an unfamiliar room. I saw a nurse taking bloodied bandages off a soldier across the room. I drifted off to sleep again and dreamed of Toby's place. I was on the floor with a girl who appeared to be Lorraine, then she turned into Gwen. I saw Billie Holiday and Duke Ellington performing on stage. My mother and father were in the audience eating curried goat. General Patton entered the club, followed by a group of MPs. He waltzed up the stairs leading to the stage. He walked in front of Billie Holiday and Duke Ellington. He was about to make a speech, when I saw Tucker blown to bits, and Charles shot. Then I saw the German soldier running for safety before being shot in half with my .50-caliber machine gun, with just his legs running away. I suddenly woke up, shivering and in a cold sweat.

I stirred in bed, feeling extremely groggy. I attempted to get up, but the dizziness overwhelmed me and I slumped back in the bed. The next morning, they removed the tube that was attached to the wound on my lower right side. I was feeling more alert when they wrapped fresh bandages on my chest and side. My leg was in a cast. Epstein made his entrance. He examined the other two patients in the room, then strode up to me. He checked my charts. "Well, the operation was a success," he said. "We got that bullet out with no problem, and you should heal up nicely. We're going to keep an eye on that leg of yours, and if it heals properly, we'll recommend that you return to active duty."

"Will I be going back to the front?" I asked.

"That's up to your company commander. I just patch you guys up and leave that up to him."

He placed the chart back on the bedpost and hurried off to other patients in the next room. I lay in my bed contemplating how I felt. On the one hand, I wanted to return to my unit with all my friends. On the other hand, I was sick of seeing my buddies getting killed, having people shoot at me, and killing other human beings. I couldn't get out of my mind that grisly scene of the German soldier being ripped apart by my machine gun, with just his legs running away, or Sergeant Tucker being blown to bits from that oncoming mortar. I fell back to sleep and continued to have nightmares of the horrors of war.

CHAPTER 34

It was late afternoon when Bubba wheeled himself to my room in a wheelchair. He had lost a little weight and needed a shave, but he looked fit. He had a cast on both legs and a small box on his lap. He offered his hand, and I reached down from my bed to shake it.

"How you doing, Bubba?" I asked.

"Fine, thanks to you and Charles. I wouldn't be here if it weren't for you guys."

"So how long have you been here?"

"Just as long as you have, about three months."

"Three months! Has it been that long?"

"It seems longer to me. I wasn't out of it like you've been. You were drifting in and out of consciousness for a while. I just got word that you're more alert now, and I had to see you before I go."

"Before you go? Where you going?"

"To some other base for therapy on my legs, then it's back to the front. But before I go, I'd like to thank you for risking your life to save mine. I feel bad about that fight we had back in England and what I said about Charles. I wish he was still around so I could thank him too." Bubba paused and looked down on his lap. "I heard he was ordered to abandon that tank, but he stayed with me."

"Yeah."

"Why do you suppose he did that?"

"I don't know, Bubba, that's a question only he could answer. I suppose that maybe he wanted to prove that he was just as good if not better than any other soldier in our unit regardless of his sexual preference."

"Well, I feel bad about what I did to you and said about him. And if anyone gives you a hard time about being gay, you just let me know and I'll take care of him."

"For the umpteenth time, Bubba, I'm not a homosexual."

"It doesn't matter none if you are or not. If anyone gives you a hard time, you just let me know. I won't be in these casts forever." I remembered that Lorraine was a friend of Bubba's cousin and asked him if he had heard from her. "No, I haven't heard from her. She probably went back to her husband," he said.

I felt like I had been kicked in the chest by a mule. "Her husband!" I exclaimed. "She was married?"

"Yeah, I thought you knew."

"No, I didn't."

"Her and her husband had been separated for a few months. They probably got back together."

"Who's her husband?"

"Some lieutenant in an ambulance company, he's stationed here in France somewhere." I sat in my bed, shocked that once again a woman let me down. She had never once mentioned her husband. Bubba didn't seem to realize how hurt I was, so I continued to hide my feelings.

He began to wheel himself out, then stopped and spun the wheelchair around. He wheeled himself back to my bedside. "I almost forgot. My mother sent this cake over for you. There's a note inside. She doesn't know how to read or write, so she had a neighbor write the letter in her words. I'll see you later." He placed the box on my lap, then wheeled himself out of the room. I opened the box and saw a chocolate cake with sprinkles and a letter on the side. I opened the letter.

Dear Mr. Jenkins

I can't thank you and that other young gentleman enough for saving my son. He told me how you and your friend kept the enemy at bay protecting him from being captured or killed. This cake is a small token of my appreciation for what you and that other soldier did. And if you're ever in Mississippi please look me up.

God bless you

Mother Jackson

I stored the letter in my nightstand and lay back on my bed. All the time Lorraine and I had spent together and the future I once thought we had meant nothing. I took a bite of the chocolate cake, then stored it away. I had no appetite for the cake or for life.

CHAPTER 35

The white soldiers who roomed with me in the hospital were distant and aloof. Only two of them, Benson and Wolf, were open and talkative. Benson was in the bed next to mine and was a jolly fellow. He was chubby and had a receding hairline. He always seemed to be laughing at something or other, and when he laughed his face would turn a bright red. He was in his mid to late thirties. Wolf, on the other hand, was a more serious guy who did a lot of reading. He was about forty-something and I wondered how a person that age got drafted into the army. An aide walked up to my bedside with a handful of letters.

"You got mail," he said.

"How much?" I asked.

He dumped all the mail he had in his hands on my lap. "All of it," he said.

"All this mail is for me?"

"Yep. This is from the time you were out on the front line, then here. It accumulated."

I couldn't believe how much mail I had received. There were letters from my parents, some from friends. There was a letter with some lipstick imprinted on the seal. My heart leapt with excitement, thinking it was from Lorraine. It sank when I saw it was from Gwen. Why is she

writing me? I thought. I went through the rest of the mail hoping there would be something from Lorraine. There was nothing. I spent the better half of the afternoon reading mail. My parents wrote that they received a letter from my company commander, Colonel Bates, informing them that I was wounded in action and unable to write. He had told them that I was expected to make a full recovery and that I'd be able to write as soon as I was well enough. I read some more letters from friends; they wrote about the Savoy, and Toby's, and how they couldn't wait for my safe return. I finished reading all the mail except for Gwen's.

The letter sat at the edge of my bed, unopened. I finally came around to opening it. A newspaper clipping was attached behind a note. It was an article from the Negro Digest. There was a semiblurred photo of a tank, with the words "Harlem Express" stenciled on the side and the number forty-two just below it. That was my tank. The figure in the picture was fuzzy, and it could have been either Tucker or me. It was a short article, stating when we were deployed and that we were an all-black tank battalion called the Black Panthers. It also stated our motto, "Come out fighting," a quote made famous by boxing champion Joe Louis when asked how he was going to fight Max Schmeling. The article continued about the battles we fought at Morville, part of the Ardennes Offense (now known as the Battle of the Bulge), the battle at the Siegfried line, and the crossing of the Rhine River.

At this time, the 761st was in Germany and moving toward Berlin with Patton's 26th Infantry.

We weren't mentioned in the Stars and Stripes or any other major newspaper, just the Negro Digest. Although I had not participated in some of those battles, I had mixed feelings of accomplishment for the battles I was in; the other feeling was guilt. I could not understand why I would have guilty feelings about killing those Germans soldiers. It was either them or me, and I chose the latter. I read the note that was attached to the newspaper clipping; it simply read, "Thought you might be interested in this. Love, Gwen."

I stared at the letter for several moments when I heard a voice beside me. "Corporal Jenkins?" I turned and saw a medium-sized black man with round, rimless glasses. I recognized him from somewhere in the unit.

"Yes, I'm Corporal Jenkins."

"I assumed you must be, seeing that you're the only colored in the room. May I sit?" "Yes, please."

He grabbed the stool that Epstein usually used and sat down. He took out a pen and pad. "I'm

Trezzvant Anderson, a war correspondent. I've been attached to your unit."

"That's where I've seen you before," I said, snapping my fingers. "I've seen you around the campsite interviewing other soldiers."

He smiled, and then continued. "I'm not sure if you're aware of it or not, but they plan to give you a Silver Star for your heroics in Morville. Do you wish to comment on that?"

"I'm getting a Silver Star?"

"Yes indeed. How do you feel about that?"

"I-I don't know what to say."

"Just say what's on your mind."

I sat in my bed, tongue-tied. The wounded white soldiers were attentive to us now, so Trezzvant pulled the stool closer to my bed and lowered his voice. "What you did was a brave act. You know that, don't you?" I just lay there and did not respond. "Do you want to speak off the record?" I nodded my head. He placed the pen and pad back in his field jacket. "What were you feeling when you were ripping your machine gun into enemy lines?" he asked.

"To be honest with you, I don't know what I felt - rage, frustration, everything is a blur. All I know is that when I saw my friend lying there dead, something came over me, an overwhelming desire to get back at the Krauts. When I look back on it now, I realize it was a mistake, exposing myself to enemy gunfire. If anyone should get a medal, it should be Charles. He chose to stay there from the start."

Trezzvant Anderson took off his glasses and placed them in his shirt pocket. "It's interesting that you brought him up. He was recommended for the Silver Star also, but the request was later withdrawn."

"Why?" I asked, surprised at this news.

"There was some type of unofficial investigation back in England at a club called Ole Brothers Place. It's a hangout for homosexuals."

"I'm aware of what it is," I intervened.

"Well, anyway, they came up with proof that Charles was gay. They already had his discharge papers drawn up. The MPs were on their way to relieve him of duty."

I sprang upright in bed, shaking my head in disbelief. "He died saving the lives of sixteen soldiers, and they didn't have the common decency to give him a medal to be buried with." I was outraged.

"What can I say? I don't make the rules, corporal. You can't be a homosexual in the army. That's just the way things are."

My blood was boiling. I was angry at the army. "You can take out the pen now. I'm ready to talk."

Trezzvant quickly reached into his pocket and withdrew his pad and pen. I began talking; everything just poured right out of me. I told him what a good soldier Charles was, how he excelled in training camp, how he held a black belt in martial arts, and how proficient he was with weapons. I went on about how he disobeyed orders to retreat to the rear so that he could stay with a wounded comrade and how he protected that wounded soldier and us, in the warehouse. I went on to tell him that it was unfair how he will be remembered - that he should not be forever known as that queer soldier, but as a hero who gave his life for his comrades-in-arms and his country. I was going to tell him more, but he held up his hand, signaling for me to stop talking. "Whoa! I can't print all this."

"Why not?" I asked.

"This is going to be printed in the Negro press, corporal. Our readers aren't interested in the mistreatment of homosexuals, but the accomplishments of our black troops."

"Charles was black," I retorted.

Trezzvant folded his pad and placed both pad and pen in his shirt pocket. "I can sympathize with the plight of your friend, corporal. I wish I could help, but my hands are tied. My editors would never allow me to print this." He stood up from the stool and shook my hand.

"If you're ready to talk about yourself getting that medal, you can get in touch with me. I'll be here for another couple of days." He walked out the room amidst the stares of the wounded white soldiers lying in their beds. Benson leaned over to me.

"I couldn't help overhearing. Your friend was a homo?" he asked.

I said nothing. I just lay back in my bed and closed my eyes.

CHAPTER 36

Benson was up jousting and joking with the other patients. The black nurse was leading the way for a lieutenant colonel; she pointed me out to him. He tucked his military hat under his arm and walked over to my bedside. He offered his right hand and I shook it.

"You're Corporal Jenkins?" he asked.

"Yes, I am," I replied. Benson and the others stopped horsing around and were attentive to us.

"I'm Colonel Tyler, and I'm here to present to you this medal. If you were in uniform, I'd pin it on you." He handed the medal to me; it was the Silver Star. He took a slip of paper from his inside jacket and began reading. "Corporal Walter Jenkins, in the heat of battle, with disregard for your own personal safety among enemy gunfire, you raced to a tank to assist a fellow soldier in holding back the Germans from overrunning your position. You aided a wounded soldier in the process, while holding the enemy back with machine-gun fire, protecting your comrades in the rear and inflicting heavy casualties on the enemy. Congratulations, soldier."

He shook my hand once more and then to my surprise and everyone else's in the room, he took his left hand and rubbed my head. I was startled that a military officer would do such a thing. Some of the nurses were embarrassed; the black nurse just looked on, shaking her head disapprovingly.

Colonel Tyler chuckled and exited the room. Benson looked at me in disbelief. There's an old saying in the South that if you rub a Negro on the head, it gives you good luck.

"Did he just rub your head?" he asked.

"Yeah, can you believe that?"

"What I can't believe is that you just sat there and took it," the black nurse said.

"What was I supposed to do?"

"You should have said something. He belittled you in front of all these people. This was supposed to be an honorable occasion, and he disrespected you like that."

"I can't just mouth off to him. He's an officer and I'm just an enlisted man. I have no right to do that."

"What you have is no balls," the black nurse said vehemently. Her comment shocked and embarrassed me even further. I could hear some of the soldiers snickering beside me.

"Who the hell do you think you are, lady? You don't know me. You have no right talking to me that way."

"All I'm saying is that if it was me and he rubbed my head like that, he would have one less hand to worry about." She turned abruptly and walked out of the room.

"You know, I believe her," Wolf said, laughing.

"If you would put a short mustache on her, she could be a black Hitler," Benson quipped.

The entire room erupted in laughter at my expense. If they send me back to the front, it wouldn't be such a bad thing, I thought. Anything is better than being here.

The following week a young captain presented me with a Purple Heart. It was a medal presented to soldiers wounded in battle. The captain gave me an honorable presentation, saying a few words before bestowing it on me. It was done respectfully, with no head rubbing involved. He saluted me and I returned the salute before he exited the room. The white patients looked on, impressed, and the Negro nurse looked on with pride. I took one more look at the Purple Heart before placing it next to the Silver Star on the nightstand.

***

I was in the hospital for about four months at this point. I was lying in bed reading about the progress of the Allied forces in Germany and was pleasantly surprised at the amount of ground they conquered at such a rapid pace. Some of the patients in the hospital returned to active duty, some stayed in the rear, some were sent back home, and others back to the front. Epstein told me that he was going to give me a few more days before recommending that I return to duty. I was getting along better with the white patients in the hospital room. Benson, Wolf, and some of the other guys would conduct wheelchair races. The white patients were warming up to me, and I to them. The suspicion and mistrust were fading away. Even a white Southerner who sat at the end of the room was beginning to be somewhat friendly to me. We played cards at the end of the day and joked around at night.

One afternoon in the middle of February, I was awakened from my nap. I looked up and saw four figures standing over my bed. I focused my eyes and realized it was my buddies from the 761st. Winston, Tank, Bubba, and another guy I recognized but forgot his name; he was light skinned with natural straight hair. He could have been biracial, but I wasn't sure. Bubba was standing with his hands cradled around his crutches. We all laughed and shook hands.

"Didn't mean to interfere with your afternoon nap," Winston kidded.

"What are you guys doing here? You're supposed to be at the front," I said.

Winston sat at the foot of the bed. He took off his glasses and slipped them into his top pocket. "They finally gave us some R and R," he said. "It's about time, too. Do you know how long they had us on the front lines?"

"Too long," Tank interjected. "It's been months since I had a decent shower."

"The way you smell, it's more like years," Bubba joked.

"Screw you. You don't smell like a bed of roses yourself." We all laughed. The biracial soldier stepped in front of the group and offered his hand.

"You probably don't remember me. I'm Scott. They assigned me to the unit right before you got shot."

"Where you from Scott?" I asked.

"Kentucky."

At that point, the black nurse strode in. The bun in her hair was let down and she had a stern look on her face. "What are you cats doing hanging around here? This ain't no Harlem pool hall," she said.

Winston sprang up from the foot of the bed, surprised by the abruptness of the nurse.

"Come on, nurse," Tank intervened. "Give us a break, will you?" We haven't seen our friend in months."

"I don't care. You're disturbing the other patients. Now go!"

"Not until we spend at least five minutes with our buddy."

"So that's the way it's going to be, huh?" She turned and stormed out of the room. Scott took out his comb and combed back his straight hair.

"Don't worry about it, guys, I'll settle her down."

"This isn't your everyday woman, man. She's a real battle-ax," I said.

He finished combing his hair and placed the comb in his back pocket. "There's not a woman in the world I can't handle," he said with a mischievous smile on his face. He walked out of the room, following her down the hallway.

"He does have a certain way with the ladies," Tank quipped.

"He has his work cut out for him with that one," I said.

Winston sat back down on the foot of the bed. "So, I heard you received the Silver Star," he said.

"Yeah, it's over there on the nightstand. Some colonel gave it to me a couple of days ago. You know, he rubbed my head when he presented it to me." Bubba, Tank, and Winston let out a gasp.

"You're kidding me," Tank said.

"God's honest truth," I said.

"It doesn't surprise me," Winston said. "They don't take us seriously. Here we are getting shot and killed, and they still treat us like house slaves. If they were serious about us, they would have given you the Medal of Honor instead of the Silver Star."

"A Medal of Honor!" I exclaimed. "They don't give that medal to Negro soldiers."

"And why not?" Winston asked. "They gave Medal of Honors to black soldiers dating back to the Revolutionary War, through every major conflict this country ever had. But now, suddenly, we don't get one in this war? Something is wrong, gentlemen."

I propped myself up on the bed. When I looked down the hall, I saw Scott talking to the black nurse. I looked around to see if any of the patients were listening to our conversation. They all seemed to be preoccupied. I lowered my voice. "Look, if they don't want to give me that medal, it's okay by me. I really don't care."

"Some of us don't feel that way, Walter," Winston said. If you risk your life in an act of patriotism and valor, then you should get the right recognition for it. You remember Sergeant Ruben Rivers, don't you?"

"Yeah, I remember him. He's half Indian."

"Well, he's dead."

"He's dead? When did he buy the farm?"

"Last month in a French town called Guebling. He was wounded and ordered to go to the rear for medical attention, but he refused and stayed with his men. He had gangrene in his leg but continued to stay, even though he knew that he might lose his leg without medical attention.

I shook my head. "I didn't know him personally, but he seemed to be a nice guy who loved the army."

Winston shook his head and continued. "He was the first to cross a makeshift bridge and led an onslaught toward the town. He and his crew were responsible for killing at least three hundred German soldiers. And he still refused to leave his men. He went head-to-head with two charging Panzers and destroyed them. The line was being overrun by an onslaught of German Tiger tanks. He provided protection, giving the other Sherman tanks a chance to retreat and regroup at the crossroads. He was later killed. His tank was destroyed, and his body almost cut in two. It was a horrible sight. I heard that Captain Williams put him in for a Medal of Honor, but no word ever got back."

"Well, in that case, he should get the medal. I don't see any reason why he shouldn't," I said.

"He's black. That's why he's not gonna get it."

It sounded cynical, but it was true. There were other acts of heroism by members of the 761st and the best anyone ever got was a Silver Star. The other thing I hated more than war was the racism in war. Winston was about to light a cigarette.

"You can't smoke in here," I said. He quickly blew out the match and placed the pack of cigarettes back in his pocket. He was about to continue his conversation, when Scott came rushing in, his face flushed.

"We've got to get out of here, man," he said excitedly.

"What's wrong?" Winston asked.

"That nurse is something else. I can't get nowhere with her."

"I thought you had a way with the ladies," I said.

"That is no ordinary lady."

The black nurse came into the room, followed by two MPs. "That's them, right over there," she said, pointing to my buddies.

"All right, the party's over you guys. Let's go," the lead MP said.

Winston slipped me a pint of cognac, placing it under the covers.

"Can't we stay just a little while longer?" Tank pleaded.

"You've stayed long enough. Come on, let's go," the second MP said.

"Can I stay?" Bubba asked, "I'm a patient."

The MPs looked at the nurse.

"He was a patient here, now he's doing therapy at the clinic. He does not belong in here," she said.

"You heard the lady. Come on, let's go."

Everyone gathered around my bed. We shook hands and bid farewell, and everyone filed out of the room, with Bubba limping behind them on his crutches. I lay back on my bed, pleasantly surprised that we were friends again. It did not seem that long ago that there was so much animosity between us. Now we were talking like old friends, the way we used to when we first met on that train ride through those Southern states.

"Hey, Walter," Benson said.

"Yeah?"

"I saw that."

"Saw what?"

"Your friend slipped you a bottle."

"I don't know what you're talking about."

"Come on. I know what I saw. You want to share it with the rest of us?" "Share what?" I asked.

"It's going to be that way, huh? Do you want me to call the colored Hitler?"

"You wouldn't."

Benson sat up on his bed. "Oh, nurse!" he shouted.

"All right, man, don't call her. You win."

Benson strolled over to my bedside. I pulled out the bottle and poured him a shot. Some of the other patients in the room saw the bottle of cognac and immediately came over. I poured each person a shot, leaving one shot for myself. Benson proposed a toast to the gallant men still fighting on the front lines, and we all drank.

CHAPTER 37

I'd been in the hospital for six months. It was early March, and most of the patients I had shared the room with were gone. Some were sent home, others were sent back to their old units. Benson was discharged for medical reasons, and Wolf went back to the front. The new white patients who replaced them did not know me and looked at me with distaste and suspicion, the same way the first group did when they first met me. I didn't talk much to this new group and pretty much stayed to myself. I read and wrote some letters and went on occasional walks on my crutches. When I returned on this particular day, I saw some letters on my bed left by the aide. I thumbed through them and saw that the usual people had written, my parents and a few friends from the old neighborhood. I was surprised to see another letter from Gwen. I was hoping to have received a letter from Lorraine, but there was none.

Gwen wrote that it was a mistake for us to break up, she was no longer seeing Country, and we should get back together again. Whatever feeling I once had for Gwen was now gone, replaced by the feelings I had for Lorraine. Why hasn't she written? I thought. The letters I wrote Lorraine were sent back, showing no forwarding address. She must have left her post in England and was sent back home to the States. I placed my crutches to the side and sat down on the edge of the bed. I was about to open the rest of my mail, when the black nurse came in.

"It's time to change those bandages," she said. I lay down, and she proceeded to take off the old bandages and put some gauze on the new bandages, expertly placing them carefully on the wounds.

"What's your name?" I asked. I was tired of referring to her as the colored Hitler, especially among this new group.

"Esther," she said. "And I'll be coming in later tonight to give you a quick sponge bath."

"Another bath? You must like what you see," I snickered.

"No, you're not big enough." She turned quickly and strode out of the room. Some of the patients overheard her and broke out in laughter. Once again, she embarrassed me. Maybe it was best to just keep my mouth shut.

***

Two more weeks passed and I was feeling stronger with each passing day. I had heard of a brothel just outside of the compound and decided to see if I could sneak out of the hospital and go off base to visit. I had accumulated some cash from back pay for the months I was hospitalized. I was still having bad dreams and feeling a little depressed, ever since they had weaned me off morphine. A visit to the local bordello was probably just what I needed. It had been quite some time since I'd been with a woman. I was always against paying for sex, but I figured I should try it this one time. All the other soldiers had done it with no complaints.

I put on my dress uniform, placed my Silver Star and Purple Heart on the chest of the jacket, and hopped out of the hospital on my crutches. I made it to the gate, where several MPs were checking incoming vehicles. They were too busy to check on GIs walking off post, so I managed to mix myself with some soldiers on their way out. The MPs just waved us on. The brothel wasn't too far, but it was hard for me to get there on my crutches. The bottoms of my armpits were getting sore. So, I hailed a cab, which took me the short distance. The driver didn't speak good English, and my French wasn't up to par, but we managed to communicate. I said, "Madam's Place," and he knew where I was going.

"Madam's Place? *Oui monsieur*," he said as we sped away. He was slim and sported an unkempt beard. He drove through traffic with ease and arrived at the destination in about five minutes. "One franc," he said.

I had no francs, only dollars. I wasn't sure what the money exchange was, so I just gave him three dollars. His eyes lit up with delight. He jumped out and opened the rear door. His English suddenly improved. "*Merci, monsieur, merci*. If you want ride back, I wait for you, yes?"

"No, you don't have to. I may be a half-hour or so."

"That's okay, I wait. You have good time, I wait." He was overly eager and pleased; I must have over-tipped him.

The door to the brothel was locked, and I knocked several times. A chubby blond woman with large breasts opened the door. "Come in, *monsieur*," she said, beaming with delight. "Welcome to Madam's Place. Have a seat."

I sat down and observed the place. The carpet was red and there were laced curtains and striped wallpaper. The hallway was to my right. The doors were closed, with red lightbulbs on top of the doorways. Two were lit. The woman sat on the couch next to me, eyeing me.

"You came at a good time, monsieur. It's a slow day," she said. "We have plenty of girls available.

What kind of girl you like? A blonde, brunette, maybe a girl of color? A gypsy, perhaps?"

I nervously lit a cigarette; I had never done this before and felt somewhat awkward. "It doesn't matter," I said.

"I will give you top of the lot. Come this way." She led me down the corridor. "We have many GIs come here, and none is ever dissatisfied."

We walked up to the last door. She knocked and said something in French. The voice inside said, "*Oui*, you may enter *monsieur*."

I opened the door to see a naked woman sitting on the bed. She stood and turned so I could have a full view of her body. If this was the top of the line, I would hate to see the bottom. It was a small room; a dresser was in the corner with a jewelry box on top. A small statue of a ballerina was on top of the box. The window was at the side. The blinds were down and the curtains closed, blocking out the sunlight. The room smelled of nicotine and cheap perfume. She seemed to have just given birth. She had stretch marks on her belly and her breasts were sagging; she looked to be still nursing. The chubby lady made her way out of the room, closing the door gently behind her.

"How would you like it, *monsieur*?" the woman asked.

"Anyway, I can get it," I responded.

"It will be twenty francs." I took out a twenty and placed it on the dresser. Her eyes popped when she saw that it was a twenty-dollar bill. She lay on the bed.

"Well, let's get started, *monsieur*. Take off your clothes. "I started to unbutton my shirt, and then stopped. I just couldn't go through with it. I turned quickly and walked out on my crutches. The chubby woman was sitting on the couch talking to another client.

"Leaving already, *monsieur*?" she asked. I said nothing and continued out the door. The taxi was still parked out front, and the cabdriver was enjoying a cigarette.

"You finish already?" he asked.

"Let's go." I said.

"That was quick." He sat behind the wheel of the cab and sped away.

"Where you go now?"

"Take me back to the base."

"You don't want to go back to the base now, *monsieur*, the night is still young."

"No just take me back to the base."

"The whores in that place are no good. I take you to a better place, with class whores. I take you, yes?"

"No, just take me back." The driver got me back in less than five minutes, and the meter read one franc again. I figured I over-tipped him the first time, so instead of three dollars I gave him two.

"*Merci, monsieur, merci*," he said. And if ever you need a cab ride again, you can reach me at this number." He handed me a card with a phone number on it. "I will show you all the nice places in town." He shook my hand and sped off in the cab. I guess I over-tipped him again. I hobbled back to the post on my crutches, and this time I was stopped by the MPs.

"How did you get off post without a pass?" one MP asked.

"I just walked off. You guys were busy."

"You know better than that corporal. You're not supposed to leave this base without a pass. I'm going to let it go this time with a warning, but next time I'm going to write you up. Understood?"

I nodded my head and continued on to the hospital. They could have made an issue out of it, but I guess they felt sympathy for a wounded soldier. On my way, I passed a building that looked like a barracks. There was a sign on the door that read "Six o-clock mass. All welcome. I looked at my watch and saw that it was ten past six and decided to walk in. I strode in the doorway and saw about eighteen white soldiers sitting on folding chairs facing a priest who was standing behind a podium. There was a giant cross behind him. He had on his standard Catholic robe, with a cross around his neck. He saw me standing in the doorway and motioned for me to come in.

"Come in, my son," he said. Being the only colored in the room, I hesitated. "Don't be shy, my son.

We are all one in God's eyes. Come in and have a seat."

I looked around for an empty seat and saw a few in the rear. I held both crutches to my side and hopped over to the chair. The priest continued with his sermon. After he finished, each soldier walked over to him and received communion. He placed white wafers in their mouths, and they drank from a tiny glass that contained wine. After the service, each soldier received a blessing from the priest, then exited the building. I remained in my seat. I didn't want to leave. I had a feeling of peace and tranquility. It was a feeling I hadn't had since arriving in the battle fields of France.

The priest spoke with several soldiers before retiring to the back room. Most of the GIs left. Some stayed, said a prayer in front of the cross, then exited the building. I was the only one sitting in the makeshift church, praying and meditating. The priest came back out. His robe was off and he was wearing his dress uniform, his chaplain insignia on his shoulders. He was somewhere in his mid-forties, with white hair that was thinning on the top. He had gray eyes and thin lips. He had rosary beads wrapped around his hand. He started to extinguish the candles in front of the podium with his fingers, when he noticed me sitting in the back row. He walked over to me.

"Is something troubling you, my son?" he asked.

"I'm not Catholic, Father, I'm Protestant."

"That is all right, son. We pray to the same God. We just worship in different ways." I saw the rosary beads around his hand and remembered the dead German soldier in the foxhole. "Is there something you want to talk about?" he asked. I saw peacefulness in his eyes and heard sincerity in his voice, and I felt I could tell this man anything.

"I've been feeling sad these last couple of weeks. I don't know if it's because they weaned me off morphine or if it's because they're sending me back to the front."

"How long have you been on morphine?"

"About two months."

"And they're sending you back to the front in your condition?"

"That's what the doctor said. He said he's going to recommend me back to duty. It's not that I'm a coward, Father, it's—"

"I never thought you to be a coward," the priest interrupted. "I see the Silver Star and the Purple Heart, which has to account for something."

"I'm just tired of the killing, Father," I continued. "Tired of the stench of death in the air. I held my best friend in my arms and watched him die. I'm tired of seeing my buddies getting blown to bits and having bullets fired at me. I'm tired of killing other human beings. I remember my first battle; it was in a little town near the coast of France. Our tanks were assembled on the outskirts. Enemy soldiers were harbored in the city, and we leveled it. When we rolled into the village, there were dead soldiers everywhere, and there was no way of telling who killed who. But the town of Morville was different."

"Different in what way?" the priest asked.

"It was up close and personal. I saw the Germans' faces as I ripped them apart with my machine gun, the panic and fear in their eyes as they fell to the ground, twitching and thrashing in agony and pain. There was one German soldier I can't forget. He was running away, and I fired on him, splitting him in two. His legs were still running without his torso. I can't get that image out of my head. All he wanted to do was get away." The priest sat down next to me. It was just the two of us in the makeshift church, sitting on folding chairs. We could hear the occasional Jeep or truck driving by outside.

"You must try to forget, my son. After all, this is war and war can be ugly."

"I wasn't in any danger; he had no weapons on him. He just wanted to run away to safety. I should have let him go."

"Did he have his hands raised in surrender to you?"

"No."

"Then under the rules of war, you had every right to shoot him."

"I should have let him get away, regardless of the rules."

"Have you discussed this matter with your superiors?"

"No."

"I am a man of God, and I shouldn't be telling you this, but if you talk with your superiors, I'm sure they would tell you that if he had gotten away, he would have lived to fight another day, killing other Americans or perhaps you."

Again, I looked into the priest's eyes and sensed sincerity in them.

"You're right," I said. "I feel like a fool for feeling this way."

"There's nothing wrong about feeling compassion for your fellow man. It shows you have a good heart. Don't lose that."

"It's just that I'm tired of this dammed war," I said.

"Watch your language, son. This is the house of the Lord."

"I'm sorry, Father," I said, slightly embarrassed. "It's just that this war has taken a toll on me."

"It's tough on everyone, my son. It's a devastating war; there's been none like it before. But you can rest assured that God is on our side."

"That's what I don't understand, Father. I shared a foxhole with, a dead German soldier. He was so young. He had rosary beads wrapped around his hands, like you. He was Catholic. I've come to realize that the Germans have Catholics, Protestants, and Lutherans, all kinds of religions. I'm sure that the clergy tell their members that God is on their side too. We're both killing each other, stating that God is on our side. Whose side is he really on?"

The priest sat silent for a moment, deep in thought. "He is no doubt on our side," he said.

"Germany is being misled by a mad dictator who has brought death and destruction throughout

Europe. Are you aware of the concentration camps that are being liberated as we speak?"

"Yes," I answered. "I've read about them."

The priest stood up and looked down at me.

"Do you think that God would be on the side of such a tyrant? A man responsible for the death of millions of innocent men, woman, and children?"

"No," I said.

He placed his hand on my shoulder. "I must go now, but you can stay as long as you want." He removed his hand. "Go with god, my son."

"I will, Father. Thank you."

He walked out the door, leaving me pondering our conversation. I must have sat there for another half-hour before deciding to head back to the hospital. As I gathered my crutches, I bowed my head and said another prayer. I limped out the door and made my way back to the hospital. A heavy load seemed to have been lifted from my shoulders; the guilt and depression was replaced with calm and ease.

CHAPTER 38

Epstein was making his daily rounds when he came to my bedside. He pulled up the stool and sat down. He pulled out a sheet of x-rays and observed them.

"Your leg isn't healing the way I would like. As you can see, the bone is crooked," he said.

"So, what's the next step?" I asked.

"I'm going to recommend that you go to a military hospital in England to get that leg reset." "Reset it how?"

"They'll break it again and hope that it heals straight the next time."

The thought of having my leg broken again was not pleasant, but going back to England meant that a discharge was just around the corner. I had survived the war. I had a slight feeling of remorse for the men who had to stay behind, but the war was almost over. I had read that the Russians were on the outskirts of Berlin and that the Allied forces had conquered all of the previously held Nazi territory.

My belongings had been placed in storage during my stay in France. I said my goodbyes to the colored nurse, Esther, and the staff and to some of the patients I had roomed with. The next morning, an aide assisted me onto a waiting Jeep. Other GIs were being escorted in two ambulances behind us. The more seriously wounded soldiers were placed on stretchers in the ambulance. It was mid-afternoon when we arrived in England. They set me up in temporary quarters with two other black GIs. It was a tight squeeze for the three of us, but we managed. One of the GIs was in the Ninety Second Infantry Division, an all-black unit that had seen combat in Italy, and the other was a mechanic, who worked on Jeeps, trucks, and tanks. Their wounds were relatively minor and they were expected to go back on duty soon. We were all pulling light duty at this time. They were waiting to get reassigned with their old units; I was waiting to get the second operation on my leg.

As I was lying in bed reading the Stars and Stripes, a special message came over the loudspeakers outside. Berlin had fallen and the Germans had surrendered. The war in Europe was officially over. There was a lot of hooting and howling in the hospital. I could hear soldiers celebrating the news outside the window. People in Jeeps and trucks triumphantly honked their horns as they drove down the road. Nurses, doctors, aides, and patients were gleefully hugging each other. The black GIs I was rooming with jumped from their bunks, and although we hardly knew each other, we cheerfully hugged and they spoke of the first thing they were going to do once they reached the States. The next day, I decided to go to Ole Brothers Place to see if I could locate Justin to tell him the bad news about Charles. I figured it would be best coming from me rather than a stranger.

I managed to catch a ride close to Ole Brothers Place and limped the rest of the way on my crutches. The streets were filled with blissful activity. Churchill had declared it Victory in Europe Day, and people were in the streets celebrating. Someone set a bonfire with a photo of Hitler on top; the flames were burning around it. Another group was throwing darts at a painting of the dictator. I managed to inch my way through the jubilant crowd. Although the English people were happy that the war was over, they were not as wild and jubilant as the crowds back in the States. I arrived at the club and tried to open the door, but it was locked, so I knocked several times. I was about to leave, when someone slowly opened the door. It was Stanley. He still looked the same odd way as when I first met him, with his hair packed with grease and the red rouge on his cheeks.

"I remember you," he said. "You're Charles' friend Walter, right?"

"In the flesh," I said, a little surprised that he remembered my name. He made a pathway for me and I hopped in on my crutches. He closed the door and observed me.

"You're hurt. Are you alright?"

"Yeah, I'm fine. Is Justin around?"

"Yes, follow me." He led me through the bar area and toward the back room. There was no activity inside the place whatsoever.

"How come this place is so dead?" I asked.

"Your military convinced our Government to close it until further notice."

"You mean they can close this place just like that?"

"What can I say? You Yanks have plenty of pull around here. Are you here to tell Justin about Charles' death?" I stopped and looked at Stanley, surprised that he knew.

"You know?" I asked.

"Yes, Justin got word about it days ago. It appears that he listed Justin as a relative. They sent a telegram to him."

Stanley led me to the back room. It was some sort of storage area for tables, chairs, and glasses. Boxes of liquor bottles were stacked in the corner. Justin was sitting at a table with a glass filled with whiskey and a half-empty bottle at the side. The shades were drawn, and the room was dark and depressing.

"He's been this way ever since he got the bad news," Stanley said. "He just sits there and drinks. He hardly says anything to anyone. Maybe you can snap him out of it." I made my way over to the table and stood in front of him.

"Hi, Justin. Remember me?" He looked up, his eyes watery and red. He nodded his head. "May I sit?" Again, he nodded his head. I pulled out a chair and gingerly sat down. The wounds in my chest and side were still sensitive. I placed my crutches at the side of the table and reached for the bottle. I poured myself a drink and took a swig.

"First off, I'd like to offer my condolences on the loss of your friend." I waited for a response, and there was none. "He was my friend too," I continued. "I know you two had something special. You both loved each other, and nobody can take that away." I waited for him to acknowledge me, but he just stared into space. I finished the rest of my drink, then stood up on my crutches. I left a piece of paper with my name and both my army and home addresses. "If there's anything you need, please don't hesitate to call me." I was about to limp out when he called out to me.

"Were you there when he died?" he asked. I limped back to the table. His eyes were still fixed on the closed shades in front of him.

"Yes, I was," I replied hoarsely. "I held him in my arms. He did a brave and noble act. He held back the enemy and prevented them from overrunning us. To me and the rest of us who were there, he was a hero."

Justin sat silent, his eyes staring straight ahead. I placed my hand on his shoulder. I wanted to say something to comfort him, but nothing came to mind. I limped out and was escorted to the main door by Stanley.

"How long has he been like that?" I asked.

"About three days now. Ever since he got that telegram."

"Keep an eye on him."

Stanley nodded his head. We shook hands, and he opened the door. Outside the jubilant crowd was still celebrating Victory in Europe Day. The bonfire was still burning, and the photo of Hitler had fallen to the bottom of the heap, the picture melting away in the searing flames. Children held hands and formed a semi-circle around the fire, gleefully singing songs about the dictator's demise. Some taverns sold drinks for half price; others gave them away for free. People were kissing and hugging. It had been six long years of war in Europe. The chaos and destruction were now over. I tried to hail a cab, when two MPs, one black, one white, approached me. A black and a white MP; that's something you rarely see. Usually they were segregated into separate units.

"You know that club is off limits to all military personnel, don't you?" the white MP said.

"No, I didn't," I lied.

"Let's see some ID," the black MP said. I showed my identification. They let me go with a warning and assisted me by hailing a cab. The taxi inched its way through the festive crowd.

The following day, I was in the mess hall having breakfast, when a sergeant came to my table and informed me that Captain Fitzgerald wanted to see me at headquarters. I couldn't understand what he was doing in England when he should have been somewhere in Germany. I figured he was probably sent here as part of an expedition team making way for the departure of American troops returning from Europe. I finished my breakfast, gathered my crutches, and went to headquarters. When I arrived, a company clerk led me to a large conference room. Captain Fitzgerald was sitting at a mid-sized table, with a first lieutenant sitting next to him. The captain had a briefcase with paperwork next to it. He was smoking his pipe as usual; the aroma of the tobacco was sweet and pleasant. I stood at attention and saluted.

"Corporal Walter Jenkins reporting, sir."

"Stand at ease, corporal." I put my crutches in front of me. I placed my hands behind my back and spread my legs slightly apart. "This is Lieutenant Baker. He'll be sitting in on this informal inquiry." I glimpsed at the lieutenant. He was young, about my age, with fair skin and a stern face. He just sat there stoically, showing no expression.

"You like the army, corporal?" Captain Fitzgerald asked.

I couldn't understand where this was leading.

"Yes, sir," I replied.

"Then why are you disobeying orders?"

"What orders would that be, sir?"

His pipe went out and he relit it with a stick match. Then he stood up from his chair and moved in front of it. He puffed on the pipe, exhaling the smoke from his nose.

"I remember a few months ago, right before we shipped off to France. I specifically told you that Ole Brothers Place was off limits to all military personnel. Then yesterday I got a report from the military police that you were in there. You deliberately disobeyed my orders. Why?"

"Sir, Charles was killed in a small town called Morville. He had a friend there who I wanted to give the bad news to."

"You mean his boyfriend, don't you?" he asked. The first lieutenant snickered, then regained his composure.

"Yes, sir," I said.

Captain Fitzgerald sat back down behind the conference table. He began fingering through the papers in his briefcase. "Let's see here. Tec Four 4 Charles Walton was going to be discharged from the military for engaging in activities unbecoming a soldier. In other words, he was a fag."

I was stunned to hear that comment coming from an officer. He was insulting my friend, who had given his life to save not only me but sixteen other soldiers. I wanted to say something in response, but I bit my tongue. "He saved the lives of fellow soldiers, sir. He refused to abandon his tank to protect a wounded soldier and covered our flank."

"And all that is commendable," Captain Fitzgerald said, but it doesn't change the fact that he was a homosexual. And no homosexuals are allowed in the military. But all that is water under the bridge. What concerns me now is you. Are you a homo?"

"No, I'm not, sir."

"Oh, you're not, Captain Fitzgerald repeated. "The last time you two were in here, he assured me that he wasn't a homo but it turned out he was lying. Are you lying too?"

"No, sir."

"You two were awfully good friends. You were seen all over the base together, going to movies and night clubs. Now if--"

"He was just my friend sir, I interrupted. "I'm a Democrat, I have friends who are Republicans, but that don't make me a Republican."

"Shut up!" Captain Fitzgerald barked. "And don't interrupt me again! Now if you are straight as you say you are, what were you doing hanging out in Ole Brothers place, a known hangout for gays?"

"I told you, sir," I said coldly. "I wanted to break the news to his friend."

Captain Fitzgerald gave me that steely-eyed look of his. His eyes were digging into me. "You mind that tone of yours, corporal," he said. "Now you still have time left in the army. I don't have proof, but I'm going to keep an eye on you. And if there's even the slightest hint that you're a fag, there will be serious consequences."

This was all I could stand; the captain was really pushing the envelope. "Permission to speak freely, sir?" I asked.

"Granted," he said.

"What the hell is it with you guys, anyway?"

The captain and the lieutenant were taken aback by my abruptness. I didn't give them a chance to respond. "Here we have a good soldier who gave his life for his country, who saved the lives of his comrades, and the only thing that concerns you is that he was a homosexual. As far as I'm concerned, you can take this inquiry or inquisition or whatever the hell you want to call it and shove it up your--"

Captain Fitzgerald sprang to his feet before I could finish, his face contorted with anger, his red face matching his hair. "You mind your tongue, soldier!" he snapped. "I gave you permission to speak freely, not to disrespect an officer. Now, as long as you're wearing that uniform, you will maintain military courtesy. Is that clear, soldier?" I said nothing. I just stared straight ahead, avoiding eye contact. "I said is that clear, soldier?" he repeated.

"Yes, sir."

"Now, I'm going to give you a chance to finish what you wanted to say. But let me give you fair warning, you be careful about the next words that come out of your mouth, because if you say what I think you're about to say, I'll throw your ass in the brig so fast it'll make your head spin. Now go ahead, proceed." I continued to look forward, avoiding eye contact with both Captain Fitzgerald and

Lieutenant Baker. "Go ahead, corporal, finish your statement."

"I got nothing else to say, sir."

The captain continued giving me that steely-eyed look of his." Get out," he said. "Get out of my sight, before I kick you in the butt so hard you'll be wearing your ass for a hat."

I didn't like that comment and was about to say something in response, like, if you think your man enough, but my better judgment took hold of me. I did an about-face, put my crutches under my armpits, and limped out of his office, defiantly not saluting him. I thought he was going to call me back in and reprimand me for not using proper military procedure, but he didn't. I made my way back to my quarters and slumped on my bed.

CHAPTER 39

I lay in bed thinking about the confrontation with Captain Fitzgerald. What I had done was stupid. I should have controlled my temper. I was months away from getting an honorable discharge, and all that was jeopardized because I opened my big mouth. Any minute, I was expecting a sergeant or an MP to enter my quarters to inform me that I was scheduled for a general court-martial for insubordination. You didn't talk back to an officer, especially in front of another officer. On the other hand, he had no right to talk so disrespectfully against Charles. He died fighting so bravely for this country, and the least they could do for him was show some degree of respect. Hell, if they want to court-martial me, they could go ahead. Charles had showed no qualms about fighting for me against Bubba. Now it was my turn to fight for him.

My leg was reset the following morning, and the doctor told me that this time it should heal properly. They gave me light duty at headquarters, doing some filing and bookkeeping. Some troops were coming through England on their way back to the States, while some were on their way to the Pacific theater to battle with the Japanese. I heard some talk that the brass was planning a major assault on the island nation and some GIs from Europe were being prepared for the Pacific. I thought of my friend Red, who was stationed somewhere out there, and wondered if he had survived. We were supposed to have a drink at Toby's if we both survived the war.

Captain Fitzgerald said nothing to me after our last meeting. I would occasionally pass him. I would salute and he would return the salute, and that would be it. I often wondered why he never pressed the issue of our last encounter in his office. Maybe because I received the Silver Star, or he just didn't want to be bothered. Or maybe he felt he was wrong. I would like to think it was the latter. Whatever the reason, I was just glad to be off the hook.

I was filing some paperwork in a cabinet in the storage area, when the company clerk came in. He was brown-skinned, with a short, cropped haircut, and a pencil behind his right ear.

"Good news, corporal," he said. "Your discharge papers came in. You're going home."

I was both surprised and ecstatic. I wasn't supposed to be discharged for another three months; the army cut me some slack. I mounted my crutches and made my way over to the clerk and vigorously shook his hand.

"I made it," I said.

CHAPTER 40

I arrived in Louisiana at a bus terminal where soldiers, marines, and sailors were milling around waiting for their buses for the journey home. Coming home from England to the Jim Crow South took some time getting used to. My bus to New York wouldn't be ready for another hour, so I needed to kill some time. I went to a store and ordered a Coke. The store clerk refused to serve me unless I went to the back. Here I was, a decorated soldier who had served his country, wearing this country's uniform, and I was being treated like a second-class citizen. I couldn't wait to get back to New York. I received my Coke and went to the colored waiting room. I saw a group of black soldiers, but none I knew. Most of my unit was still in Germany preparing for their journey to the states.

I finished my Coke and decided to have a second one. On my way to the rear of the store, I saw a group of white soldiers congregating next to the bus entrance. I continued about my business, when one of the soldiers shouted at me.

"Hey, corporal!"

Oh no, I thought. Are these guys going to give me trouble? I turned and saw a tall beefy white man walking toward me.

"Don't I know you?" he asked. I looked closer and realized who he was. It was Ben O'Brian, the guy who had started the fight back in that pub in England. What are the odds of me seeing him again, out of hundreds of thousands of soldiers? It had to be one in a million. But there he was, chewing gum and sipping a Coke. I wanted to ignore him and continue on my way, but he caught up with me.

"I know you, you're that guy from the pub," he said.

"Yeah," I responded. I was about to walk away.

"You're with that tank battalion, the Seven Hundred and Sixty-First, aren't you?" "Yes."

"I'm with the Twenty-Sixth Infantry. You guys backed us up over there in Europe." I looked at him and realized he didn't want to start trouble. "I was over in Ardennes, Saar, and Gruebling before we worked our way to the Siegfried line and into Germany.

One of your tanks saved a group of friends of mine over in Gruebling.

"I didn't get a chance to go that far. I was wounded in a town called Morville," I said.

"Morville, yeah, I heard there was some heavy fighting there. Town got cut off by the Krauts for several hours." He looked down at my leg and saw my cane. "Got wounded in the leg?"

"I got shot in the leg, chest, and side. I almost died."

He looked at my leg once more. He took a drink from his bottle of Coke, then smiled. "Well, see you around."

He walked back to his assembly of friends. I continued to the rear of the store to receive another Coke. When I returned, my bus was already loading. I limped over with my cane and got in line.

The bus driver was taking tickets from the passengers. When he got to me, he stared for a moment.

"You have to sit in the rear, boy," he said. I rolled my eyes in disgust. Here we go again, I thought. Welcome home. I was about to say something, but Ben intervened.

"Come on, give the guy a break, will ya."

The bus driver gave Ben a disgusted look. "That's what the rule says. He goes to the back."

"Do you see those medals on his chest? He fought over in France, got wounded fighting for this country. Let him sit up front with me."

The bus driver looked on the medals on my chest. "Hey, look, buddy. I don't make the rules around here, all right?"

"You can bend them a little, can't you?" Ben said. "Come on, give this guy a break. Look at his leg. It's gonna be tough for him to make it up that aisle."

"You don't mind him sitting next to you?" the bus driver asked.

"I would be honored if he sat next to me."

The driver looked at Ben, then me. He shook his head and shrugged his shoulders. "Suit yourself," he said. "I guess I can do it this one time."

I wanted to tell the bus driver not to do me any favors, but I appreciated Ben's gesture and sat in front with him. He was heading for New York also. He was from Long Island and had been drafted around the same time as me. It was a long journey back to the city, but we talked a lot, which helped make the time slip away. It turned out he was quite a charming fellow. It was hard to believe that a year ago we were at each other's throats in that pub in England.

We swapped war stories and joked around some. There's no racism on the battlefield, I thought. When the bullets are flying and the bombs are falling, you don't care what color the guy's skin is next to you, or his sexual preference. All that matters are what uniform he wears. When we returned to New York, I knew that he would go to his neighborhood and I to mine, and we'd live our separate lives. But for that one instant on the battlefield when we were backing the white infantry and they in turn were backing us, we were one.

CHAPTER 41

I got a job at the post office after my discharge. Originally, I wanted to get my old job back at the Waldorf, but Mr. Riley was no longer the manager there, and the new manager knew nothing of the promise Mr. Riley had made about getting my job back after my discharge. It was probably for the best. I worked nights at the post office and went to school during the day. I became a minister about five years after my discharge. Ever since I had that heart-to-heart with that Catholic priest back in England, I realize that was my calling. I had a church on Lenox Avenue near Toby's Place, my old hangout. I still worked at the post office and eventually married a woman who sang in the choir. We raised four children, two boys and two girls.

I still bore the scars of the gun-wounds I received in combat. I walked with a slight limp, especially when we had inclement weather. I went to a few of the 761st reunions, but I stopped after I became a minister. In 1966, I made a trip to France, to the Normandy American Cemetery in Colleville-Sur-Mer, where most of the GIs who fought in France were buried. I couldn't afford to take my wife and kids, so I made the journey myself. I remembered the days when you could only make the trip by boat, but aviation really made some strides over the years. It used to take four days or more by ship; now I could make it to Europe in six hours by jet.

When I arrived in France, it was a cold and dreary day. I took a cab to the cemetery. This time I knew the money exchange and did not over-tip the cab driver. When I entered the gates of the cemetery, I noticed white stoned crosses marking the gravesites, as far as the eye could see. With some help from the caretaker, I located Charles' grave. I had a warm feeling of the camaraderie we shared on and off the battlefield. I had a sense of guilt for the way I had treated him when I first found out he was gay. I'm supposed to be a minister, but I don't despise anyone's lifestyle. Love the person, hate the sin, I always thought. Besides, who am I to judge?

I took my Silver Star and placed it on top of the stone cross. "You deserve this medal more than me, Charles." I said. "I'll never forget what you did and the sacrifice you made." I saluted the monument, bowed my head, and said a silent prayer.

CHAPTER 42

I kept in touch with Winston and Bubba, and although the unit was disbanded in the fifties, we went to all the reunions that the 761st had up until I became a minister and stopped going. It didn't seem appropriate that a man of God should be out celebrating and boasting about battles and victories at the cost of human life. I just wanted to put the past behind me and forget about the war. The year was 1996. I was seventy-four then, and a lot had happened since my discharge from the army in 1945: the integration of the military forces, the Civil Rights Act, the Voting Rights Act, and Jackie Robinson, who used to be with the 761st, becoming the first African American to play Major League Baseball

On January 24, 1978, after an investigation clearly showed that racism had played a part in the 761st not getting the recognition they deserved, on January 24, President Jimmy Carter signed orders awarding the 761st Tank Battalion the Presidential Unit Citation for extraordinary heroism. In 1994, Fort Hood headquarters was designated 761st Tank Battalion Avenue. In 1995, the Main

Processing Unit was named in honor of Ruben Rivers. In late August, I received a call from Winston, telling me that all former members of the 761st were invited to a celebration in Killeen, Texas, a town near Fort Hood. I declined, and so did many others. It was hard to forget the mistreatment we received when stationed there. But Winston and a group of others went. When they came back, they told stories of how well they were treated. They received a key to the city from the mayor, and a street named after our battalion. Some young town folks even approached Winston and apologized for the way we had been treated by their parents and grandparents during those turbulent years. Hearing this made me realize that times were really changing.

In 1993, an investigation was launched, and it was proven again that there was racism in the ranks of the military when it came to issuing the Medal of Honor, the highest honor given to an

American soldier. There were 433 medals issued to soldiers during World War II, but none of the 1.2 million African Americans who served received the prestigious honor. The Pentagon established a committee of military historians to search through the archives to see if any black soldiers had been considered. In 1996, nine names of soldiers who should have been considered came up. Seven were eventually accepted. Ruben Rivers of the 761st was one of them.

On January 13, 1997, on my seventy-fifth birthday, a ceremony was held for the seven African

American soldiers to present them with this prestigious award. Only one man, Lieutenant Vernon J. Baker, was still alive to receive the honor. He had been with the Ninety-Second Infantry Division.

Although I had stopped attending the 761st reunions, I made it a point to go to this ceremony. A group of World War II veterans were invited to the Oval Office to honor the occasion. Relatives of the deceased honorees were standing in front of the audience. President Bill Clinton stationed himself behind a podium with the presidential seal on the front. He made a short speech, then began reading the names of the recipients and their heroic deeds. If Charles hadn't been discharged for being gay, his name would have been read. I received notice that I was approved for the prestigious award, But I declined the honor, It would have been accepting an award for killing and maiming other human beings, and being a man of God, it would have gone against everything I was taught and believed in.

I had heard that Tank passed away several years back. I wished that he could have been there for the occasion. Winston and Bubba were standing next to me. Winston's glasses were thicker, and he had patches of gray in his hair. He had grown a mustache that was completely gray. Bubba had put on some weight, and his hair was white. He still looked somewhat fit for a man his age. As for myself, I was bald on top with gray hair on the side, and I wore a hearing aid that I had to adjust so I could hear the president speak. Tears welled up in my eyes when I thought of Charles, Bay Bay, Tucker, Rivers, and others who paid the ultimate price for fighting that war so long ago. President Clinton adjusted his papers on the podium and came to the final recipient:

"And to Sergeant Ruben Rivers; of the 761st Tank Battalion, for extraordinary heroism in action during the fifteenth to nineteenth of November 1944 toward Guebling, France. Though severely wounded in the leg, Sergeant Rivers refused medical treatment and evacuation. He took command of another tank, and advanced with his company in Guebling the next day. Repeatedly refusing evacuation, Sergeant Rivers continued to direct his tanks to fire at the enemy's position through the morning of nineteen November, 1944. At dawn, Company A's tanks began advancing toward Bougaktroff but were stopped by enemy fire. Sergeant Rivers, joined by another tank, opened fire on enemy tanks, covering Company A as they withdrew. While doing so, Sergeant River's tank was hit, killing him and wounding the crew. Staff Sergeant River's fighting spirit was an inspiration to his unit and exemplifies the highest tradition of military service."

Through the applause, President Clinton handed the medal to the sisters of Ruben Rivers.

After the president issued the medals to the descendants of the fallen heroes, a group of us milled around outside a conference area. Coffee and donuts were served, and World War II veterans stood around, conversing with each other in their veteran uniforms. There were black veterans from the 92nd and the 761st. We had our Black Panthers insignia on our right shoulders with our motto, "Come out fighting," underneath. I did not wear the veteran uniform. I wore a dark-blue pin striped suit with my white collar around my neck. I and other ex-soldiers wore name tags on our chests so we could be identified. Aging over the years changed our features. I sensed someone observing me as I was conversing with Bubba and Winston. I looked up and saw a woman with gray-and-white hair staring at me. Her hair was thick and combed back. She looked to be in her late sixties or early seventies. She walked toward me in a dignified manner. When she got close enough, she read my name tag.

"Walter Jenkins!" she exclaimed. "I thought that was you."

I glanced at her name tag, and it read "Lorraine Carter." We briefly hugged, then she quickly hugged Bubba and Winston.

"It's so good to see you guys," she said cheerfully. "How have you been?"

"Fine." I responded. "You're still looking good after all these years."

"Oh, stop it now. These old bones of mine are seeing their last miles. So, how's Annabelle, Bubba? I haven't seen her in ages."

"She passed a few years back," Bubba said.

"Oh, I'm sorry to hear that."

"She died from a stroke. We can only be thankful that she went quickly."

We spoke for a few more moments, reminiscing about old times in the army, when Bubba and Winston excused themselves. Lorraine and I were left alone. I felt a little awkward standing there alone with an old girlfriend.

"I don't know about you, but I could use a cup of coffee," I said.

"So, can I," she said smiling.

We worked our way through the crowd to a table that was lined with boxes of Dunkin Donuts and a coffee percolator in the middle. I poured a cup for her, then for myself. I inspected the donuts and decided on a glazed honey dipped. She declined and settled for just the coffee.

"It's been a long time," I said again, not knowing anything else to say.

"It has been," she said, sipping her beverage. "All right, Walter, I'm going to come right out with it. It's been many years, but I felt bad about not responding to your letters."

"Forget about it, Lorraine. It was another time and place. We're both married now, with children and grandchildren."

"I was separated from my husband when we first met," she continued, "and you stirred things in me that no man had in years. When I went to Avon mouth, I found out you had shipped out to France. I wanted to get in touch with you, but—"

"You don't have to explain, Lorraine," I interrupted.

"I feel that I should. I tried to get in touch with you, but my husband wanted us to get back together, so for the sake of our marriage, I decided to give it one more try. I tried writing a letter, but you had already shipped back to the States and I didn't know your forwarding address." "How many children do you have?" I asked.

"I have two daughters. They're all grown up now, married with children of their own."

"And your husband?"

"We divorced about twenty years ago. But enough about me. Look at you, a minister! How long have you been a man of the cloth?"

The chattering of veterans got louder and there seemed to be some kind of commotion at the center of the room. President Clinton made his entrance. He began conversing with the veterans, shaking their hands and having his picture taken with them. I turned my attention back to Lorraine.

"About forty-four years now. I'm going to retire in a couple of years, as soon as I find a successor."

"How long have you been married?" she asked.

"Forty years. I have four kids, two boys, and two girls." She continued looking at me and my collar.

"The Reverend Walter Jenkins. I knew there was something special about you the first time we met." President Clinton was getting closer to Lorraine and me, and he made his way up to us.

"Hello, Reverend, were you in the military?" he asked.

"Yes, I was, Mr. President. The Seven Hundred Sixty-First Tank Battalion."

"And how about you, madam?"

"I was with the Six Thousand Eight Hundred Eighty-Eighth Postal Division, Mr. President." He stood straight and tall, looking into our eyes. He smiled and shook both our hands with a firm handshake.

"Thank you for your service," he said. He continued to walk with people swarming around him, wanting to shake his hand or take a picture with him.

"Well, I must be going, Walter. It's been a pleasure seeing you again." She drained the rest of her coffee, threw the empty paper cup into a small container, and started for the exit.

"You take care of yourself now, Lorraine," I said. She waved and resumed walking out of the room with that dignified walk of hers. There she goes, I thought. Out of my life as quickly as she came into it. I finished the rest of my coffee, then went to see if I could find Bubba and Winston.

CHAPTER 43

About two months later, I received a phone call from a reporter from Ebony magazine who was doing an article about the 761st. He had already interviewed some of the other veterans from my unit, and my name had come up several times. I declined to be interviewed so he asked me if I had any photos from that period that he can borrow. I saw no harm in it so I made an appointment for him to come by later in the day. I was in the church office when he stopped by. He was a short, stocky man with a full beard and a short, neatly trimmed afro. I gave him some photos that I had managed to find in the attic. There was one picture of Charles, Winston, and me taken in front of a captured German Panzer. Also, some photos of blown-up buildings, and Winston displaying a Nazi flag. The reporter eagerly took the pictures, promising that they would be returned on Thanksgiving eve.

I was sitting in my study, in my modest but immaculate home, going over my sermon for Sunday service when my wife came in and told me a reporter was waiting to see me in the living room.

When I went into the living room, I saw him admiring the pictures of me and my family on the wall.

He handed me the pictures I had given him and told me that one or two would be in the magazine. He asked me if I would reconsider doing an interview if he gave me anonymity. Again, I declined. He bid me farewell and left my house. My wife, Joanne, was standing at the walkway leading to the kitchen, shaking her head disapprovingly.

"What's wrong?" I asked.

"Why don't you do the interview? There are a lot of people who don't know the accomplishments of your unit. It's something you should be proud of."

"I'm proud of what I've accomplished right now. Besides, how is it going to look, a man of the cloth talking about himself killing and maiming fellow human beings?"

"I'm sure people would understand, Walter. That was a long time ago."

"I don't want to do it. I don't want to bring up the memories of what happened in the past. I just want to forget about it."

Joanne simply shook her head. She wiped her hands with a towel and returned to the kitchen. She was a slender, light-skinned woman. She was slim when we first met, and although we have four children, she has not gained a pound. Although she has aged, I still see the beautiful bright woman I met forty years ago in the choir.

It was Thanksgiving Day. All my kids and grandkids were at the house. My kids were grown, ranging in age from thirty-eight to forty-seven. My grandkids ranged in age from five to seventeen. It was pleasant having my family over, my little grandchildren running around, not a worry in the world. I was sitting at my desk in my study, finishing up my Sunday sermon, when I decided to have a drink. I went to the hallway closet adjacent to the kitchen. I heard some mumbling coming from the kitchen, so I adjusted my hearing aid. My wife was speaking with our oldest son, Malik. He was light-skinned like his mother and taller than me.

"I just don't understand why he doesn't want to do the interview. It's all part of our history," Malik said.

"You have to understand," Joanne said, "It's something he doesn't like to talk about. He only vaguely told me about what happened over there when we first got married."

Malik sat down at the kitchen table, shaking his head in dismay. The table was already set. The silverware was neatly distributed atop the napkins, and the turkey was placed in the middle of the table. My younger grand-kids were playing in the backyard, while my teenaged grand-kids were in the living room playing Nintendo.

"I just don't understand it," Malik reiterated. "It's something he should be proud of, something

African Americans would be proud to hear about."

"You have to understand your father, Malik," Joanne said. "Not only does it bring up bad memories, but he's a minister."

"So, what?"

"He feels guilty for the loss of life he caused."

"It was war, Mom. Plus, it was a long time ago, before he became a minister."

"I'm going to have to agree with Malik," my youngest daughter, Inez, said. "It's all part of history that Daddy was part of. It should be told."

"I don't want to hear anything more about this," Joanne said. "You will respect your father's wishes."

I poured my drink, whiskey with a lot of ice. I returned to my study and sat down at my desk. I pondered what was said in the kitchen and was reminded of what the army recruiter had told me. Why should I be a cook when I could be something to be proud of, a member of the first all-black tank battalion? My wife shouted my name, informing me that dinner was ready. I walked into the kitchen with my drink in my hand. Everyone was sitting at the dinner table eager to begin eating. The kitchen had a nice aroma of turkey, stuffing, candied yams, rice, and vegetables. The apple pie was cooling off on the kitchen counter. I sat down, and we all held hands while I said grace. After dinner, my grandkids sat in front of the television while the rest of us sat in the living room. Malik told a story about an encounter he had at his job. After he finished, I made an announcement.

"I'm about to do something that I refused to do for over forty years," I said. "I'm going to tell you what took place during my years in combat over in Europe." Everyone in the living room was astonished by this. "I always maintained that the war I was involved in was something I did not want to talk about. But hearing what was said in the kitchen earlier made me realize that it's something that must be told before I die."

Malik abruptly stood from his seat. "I'm going to call that reporter," he said.

"No!" I exclaimed. Only family are going to hear this story. If you want to relay it to Ebony later, that's your prerogative."

All the family members, including the little children, filed into my study. I sat behind my desk while the adults managed to gather chairs from the kitchen. The grandkids sat snugly next to the fireplace, the fire burning nice and evenly. This reminded me of the time I was in England with Bay Bay, Winston, Bubba, Tank, and Charles, eager to hear the story from that old English gentleman about the Zulu wars. I filled my glass with ice, then poured some more whiskey; I took a sip and looked up at the anxious faces hanging onto my every word.

I started from the very beginning, when I got my draft notice. I told them about Red and the encounter we had at the bar, and the hard training we endured in boot camp. I told them how we were mistreated in Louisiana at Fort Claiborne and at Fort Hood, Texas. I told them about having to sit in the back of the bus and how German prisoners were treated better than us. I told them about Bubba, Bay Bay, Tank, and Winston. I briefly mentioned Charles's homosexuality. I told them about the barroom brawl at the English pub.

Then I came to the hard part, the battlefields of France. I took a long sip from my glass, then continued. I told them about the dead German soldier I shared a foxhole with, the battle along the coast of France, the Saar campaign, and then the battle of Morville. I told them about Charles' bravery and how he was killed. I saw some grimaces on my sons' and daughters' faces when I told them in detail about the German soldier I cut in half with my .50-caliber machine gun. I finished up by telling them about the presidential award we received as a unit and individually. I finished my story and looked up at the awed faces of my audience. I drained the rest of my drink.

"Any questions?"

"When you were in that town, how many soldiers did you kill?" Malik asked.

"I'm not sure. If I had to give a number, I'd say not more than seven."

"Did General Patton really make a speech in front of the black battalion?" my youngest son, Paul asked.

"Yes."

"What's a homosexual?" my youngest grandson, Jason, asked.

"When you're old enough, I'll tell you."

"Who's Lorraine?" Joanne asked.

"She's a girl I met in England. She was with the army post office."

"When you were deployed to England, did all African American soldiers stay in the lower quarters of the ship?" my oldest daughter, Joyce, asked.

"Pretty much. There were some who ventured upstairs, but not many."

"It's funny you never mentioned this Lorraine woman before," my wife said.

"It was a long time ago. We only dated briefly."

"What ever happened to your white friend, Red?" Malik asked.

"I don't know. I tried to get in contact with him, but no one knows his whereabouts. We never did have that drink together at Toby's like we planned."

I spent more than an hour answering questions until finally we decided to call it a night. Everyone left, leaving my wife and me all by ourselves in a home that once had so much life in it. I helped her with the dishes, and just when we were about to turn in, she looked at me. "Walter?"

"Yes, hon?"

"Was this Lorraine woman pretty?"

CHAPTER 44

Many years have passed, and so much has happened personally and politically. I retired from the church and settled down at home. In 2008, the first African American president was elected. I never thought I'd live to see the day. My wife passed in 2005, never seeing that great day in American history. I'm ninety-two now and living in a nursing home. There are not too many veterans from that era in the home. Most of the residents here are in their early eighties, too young to have fought in World War II. Either all my army buddies have died, or I lost track of them. Bubba drowned in a river in Mississippi, and the last I heard from Winston, he moved in with a daughter in another state and then I lost track of him. That was three years ago.

I'm just sitting here in my chair in my room, watching television. There is a TV in the recreation hall where a group of us get together to be entertained by the box, but my son thought that every now and then I would like to have some privacy. So, the family got together and bought this nice flat-screen television for my room. I've been here ever since.

EPILOGUE

Walter looked up and saw Joseph Shapiro jotting down everything he had just said.

"You got everything?" Walter asked.

"Pretty much. What I didn't get the tape recorder picked up. I guess these wraps everything up." Joseph stood up from the bed and began putting the tape recorder in the case. He folded the microphone and neatly packed it in the side slot. He put away his pen and pad, then slid his hat on his head. He offered his hand to Walter and they shook. "It's been a pleasure, Mr. Jenkins. If I need a follow-up, I'll get back in touch with you."

"So, when is the book coming out?"

"Hard to say. I have a few more people to interview from your unit. Maybe you might know some of them?"

"I doubt it. Most of the people I knew are dead. I only knew everyone else in my unit in passing."

"Well, as soon as I get a definite date for the book, I'll get in touch. By the way, I was deeply touched by the friendship you had with Charles. Back in those days, people weren't open-minded about homosexuality. It's hard to believe that at our first meeting, when you refused to be bathed by a man, I thought you were a homophobe."

"Well, in truth, I was acting like a dick."

Joseph smiled. A man from the 1940's using a twenty-first century expression. He glanced at the television and noticed a caption underneath Wolf Blitzer of CNN speaking to a fellow reporter. The television was muted, but the caption said that the Supreme Court had ruled in favor of gay marriage. Joseph rushed back to the bed and sat down on the edge. "Please, Mr. Jenkins, could you turn that up?"

Walter reached for his remote and turned up the volume, and to the surprise of both men, they learned that the Supreme Court had ruled that all fifty states must abide by the right of homosexuals to marry. People outside of the court were cheering and celebrating. Joseph had tears of joy in his eyes.

"I don't believe it," he said. "I never thought I'd live to see the day. How do you feel about this, Mr. Jenkins? You've lived through a lot, the Depression, World War II, civil rights, the first black president. How do you feel about these recent events involving gay men and women?"

Walter continued staring at the television, remembering his best friend Charles. "It's been a long time coming."

AUTHOR'S NOTES

Like a lot of people, I never knew of the heroics of the 761st Tank Battalion. As a young black man who grew up in the sixties, I had heard of an African American tank battalion in World War II, but I never knew the details of the battles and struggles they endured. I had always thought that they were never involved in any serious battles or that they were only mascots. I was amazed to find out, through research, that the battles they were involved in included the Battle of the Bulge. Walter, Charles, Bubba, Tank, and Winston are characters that I envisioned against the backdrop of this amazing group. I got all my knowledge of the 761st by researching the computer and reading two books: *Brothers in Arms*, by Kareem Abdul-Jabbar and Anthony Walton, and *Patton's Panthers*, by Charles W. Sasser. These two outstanding books give details of the battles, the hardships, and the accomplishments of these soldiers. I recommend both books.

Printed in the USA
CPSIA information can be obtained
at www.ICGtesting.com
LVHW071018291124
797928LV00001B/3